Confronting Authority

CONFRONTING AUTHORITY

Reflections of an Ardent Protester

Derrick Bell

BEACON PRESS
Boston

Beacon Press
25 Beacon Street
Boston, Massachusetts 02108-2892

Beacon Press books
are published under the auspices of
the Unitarian Universalist Association of Congregations.

99 98 97 96 95 94   8 7 6 5 4 3 2 1

Text design by Diane Levy

Library of Congress Cataloging-in-Publication Data

Bell, Derrick A.
    Confronting authority: reflections of an ardent protester /
Derrick Bell.
        p.   cm.
    Includes bibliographical references.
    ISBN 0-8070-0926-1
    1. Harvard Law School—Faculty—Recruiting. 2. Harvard Law
School—Faculty—Selection and appointment. 3. Afro-American
women law teachers—Selection and appointment—Massachusetts—
Cambridge. 4. Bell, Derrick A. 5. Law teachers—Massachusetts—
Cambridge—Biography. 6. Dissenters—Massachusetts—Cambridge—
Biography. I. Title.
KF292.H325B35   1994
340'.071'17444—dc20   94-13420
                            CIP

We must complain. Yes, plain, blunt complaint,
ceaseless agitation, unfailing exposure of dishonesty
and wrong—this is the ancient, unerring way to
liberty, and we must follow it.

—W. E. B. Du Bois

CONTENTS

CONTENTS

PREFACE

Dick Gregory reports that back in the early 1960s he mounted a one-person campaign against racial discrimination in the Olympic Games. As part of this protest, he flew from San Francisco to Los Angeles one morning after a long night of work and carried a picket sign decrying racism outside the Coliseum where Olympic trials were being held. The sun was hot, and the spectators and even a group of black athletes streamed by, ignoring Gregory and his sign. Disappointed, Gregory disposed of his sign and headed back for the airport. He had to work that night. Although disheartened at the time, many years later he learned that sociologist Harry Edwards's father had taken him to those Olympic trials, that he had noticed Gregory walking in the heat carrying his sign, alone and unnoticed. Edwards determined right then to organize the action that resulted in the famous protests by black athletes at the 1968 Olympic Games.[1]

At its essence, the willingness to protest represents less a response to a perceived affront than the acting out of a state of mind. Challenges to those in power are not necessarily motivated by belligerence or hostility, though these emotions may well be present. Nor are retaliation or revenge the major impulses that lead an individual to challenge an injustice even when its origin is a more powerful individual or institution. Often, the desire to change the offending situation, which is often beyond our reach, may be an incidental benefit and not the real motivation. Rather, those of us who speak out are moved by a deep sense of the fragility of our self-worth. It is the determination to protect our sense of who we are that leads us to risk criticism, alienation, and serious loss while most others, similarly harmed, remain silent.

Protest that can rescue self-esteem is of special value to black Americans in a society where overt discrimination and unconscious acts of racial domination pose a continual threat to both well-being and mental health. I recognize, of course, that the need of many whites to use race as a measure of their superiority is in itself a most serious manifestation of personal inadequacy, a deficiency worsened rather than remedied by racially discriminatory beliefs and actions. Getting beyond their obsession with racial preference, and confronting the real barriers to opportunity and equality that burden whites, will bring real benefits to themselves and to blacks as well.

For each individual, there are specific responses rather than generic formulas that can be invoked at every confrontational crisis. Although the decision to confront rather than conform is intensely personal, I believe that sharing my own confrontational experiences may provide a pattern of situation and response that others can identify with and relate to their own lives. What I have done here is set out my major confrontations with persons in authority. I have tried as honestly as I can to include my motivations and methods, my successes and failures, my fears and how I resolved them by balancing the risks of protest with the possibility of success and the certainty of protecting my sense of who I am.

This book does not aim to convince readers that a passive response to harassment and ill treatment is always wrong, a confrontational one always appropriate. Few, if any, of us could survive in modern society by challenging every slight, every unfairness we experience or witness. I do believe, though, that most people are too ready to accept unwarranted and even outrageous treatment as part of the price of working, of getting along, even of living. I also believe people are being hurt in very real ways, not only as a result of what others do to them, but also by what they do to their self-esteem when they submit to maltreatment. When considering how to respond to abuse in the workplace, it is all too easy to magnify the risks of confronting the abuser while diminishing the possibility that a strong response will either end the abuse or provide the satisfaction of having made clear that abusive treatment is unacceptable.

Even for those who are considering confrontation as an alternative to passive acceptance, there are no "Ten Easy Steps" to adopting a more aggressive stance to the indignities suffered by individuals or groups you wish to defend. There are, though, certain considerations, cautions as well as tactics, that can help in arriving at the decision to confront and in implementing the challenge to wrongful treatment. My experiences may be more a cautionary tale than a call to confrontative colors. If the way of the peacemaker is hard, that of those who individually challenge authority is even harder. Peace is viewed as a virtue even by those who reject it. Protesters, though, are likely to be denounced as troublemakers by both opponents and friends.

Of course, I will be pleased if my experiences encourage readers to consider openly confronting wrongs that afflict their lives and the lives of others. I wish I could guarantee that taking risks, even making sacrifices to protest unfair policies or conditions, will invariably bring relief. I can't. I have been very fortunate—thus far; but I know that speaking out can result in lost jobs, ruined opportunities, and damaged careers. During a period of economic hardship and an ever tightening job market, this is no small risk. Taking a stand, however, can also end harassment and win respect. It can bring about the change you seek for yourself and also for others facing similar hurdles. In addition, an unexpected victory may occur in an unexpected way long after a protest is made and forgotten.

In recounting the stories of others whose willingness to face dangers and make sacrifices have encouraged and inspired my far less risky confrontations with those in authority, I hope my efforts and this book will serve as a small testament to the countless individuals, young and old, black and white, who were killed, beaten, jailed, or professionally destroyed for integrating lunch counters, schools, buses, and voting rolls, for marching, speaking, and gathering in the cause of racial justice.[2]

Finally, candor requires that I state at the outset what I hope this book will make clear. There are many perspectives on any serious protest. The protester is not a prophet. Confrontations with authority test the legitimacy of power. They are neither right nor wrong in some absolute or definitive sense. To illustrate this point, I have employed an allegorical story as a contrapuntal introduction to each of my narrative chapters. My fable of "The Citadel" should provide a broader view of the events reported here, events that, swayed by the temptations of advocacy, I may tend to portray in sharply defined terms of right and wrong. The protester, while seeking always to carry the banner of truth and justice, must remember that the fires of commitment do not bestow the gift of infallibility. Even the most well-meaning can err in the mission of good, can worsen conditions they seek to reform. An important part of the challenge of confronting authority is to recognize human limitations in all these things, consider them along with the risks, and then, despite all, move forward and face powers greater than your own.

I concede that it is possible, but it is hard for me to imagine how an individual can mount a protest challenging established power without the close and continuing support of at least one other person. Throughout all my protests, Jewel, my wife of thirty years, was my fiercely loyal companion. Even during an almost decade-long battle with breast cancer, she continued to provide always welcome support and not-always heeded advice. Jewel died in early August 1990, just before the start of the first year of my protest leave against Harvard Law School.

Jewel was a unique human being. In our marriage, she had served as sanctuary. Some of my actions—including the protest leave—tried her patience, but she was never less than fiercely loyal. She resented deeply Harvard's refusal to recognize my work, and finally accepted my leave-without-pay protest as a costly but necessary way of exposing the school's hypocrisy.

Several years earlier, long before her illness, Jewel had declared, "If I should die first, I hope you will marry again." To my puzzled look, she said simply, "it will be a compliment to me." I didn't understand until her death what she meant. I missed Jewel and realized that marriage to her was more than a status. For us, it had become a state of preferred being. Remarriage would be an affirmation of our relationship.

In a miracle of good fortune that surpasses both belief as well as any entitlement on my part, I met Janet Dewart. An editor with long experience in television and public relations, she called seeking permission to use one of my fictional stories in the National Urban League's annual publication, *The State of Black America*. Janet was the book's editor and we worked together by telephone, going over drafts of an Introduction that would appropriately fit my fictional work into a volume of social science essays.[3] Our friendship developed through telephone conversations for several weeks. We met in January 1991 and married in June 1992. Janet, like Jewel, displays an understanding and support for my past (and present) confrontations that is not only welcome but essential for one committed to individual protest.

I wish to acknowledge the generous financial support I received for this project from Lynn Walker, director of the Rights and Social Justice Program at the Ford Foundation. In addition, thanks to the generosity of the New York University Law School and its dean, John Sexton, I was granted a scholar-in-residence position during the 1993–94 school year. Ms. Linda Singer, a former student and a leader of the Harvard Coalition for Civil Rights, worked closely with me on this book for several months. Her research, writing, and editing contributed enormously to the final work. Ms. Singer contacted other Harvard Law grads who, as students, were activists in the diversity campaign. John Bonifaz, Keith Boykin, and Lucy Koh, among others, provided their stories about the events from 1990 to 1992. Phoebe Hoss, the editor of two of my earlier books for another publisher, interrupted work on a book of her own to give this manuscript the benefit of her seasoned eye and sharply pointed pen. Wendy Strothman, publisher of Beacon Press, approached me with the idea for this book, and Senior Editor Deborah Chasman at Beacon shepherded this project through countless drafts and provided overall editing supervision and direction. Several persons read various drafts and made helpful comments. They include Carter Bell, Janet Dewart Bell, Deborah Creane, Mary Kimble, Suzette Malveau, Charles Ogletree, and Lida Rodriguez-Tasef.

Note: Conversations quoted in the text reflect the general tenor rather than verbatim statements of what was said.

Confronting Authority

The Fame for Failure Paradox

*F*rom a distance, the Citadel resembles Camelot. Located high on an impressive mountain, the Citadel is often invisible in the mists and clouds that abound at such altitudes. But on a sunny day, particularly after rains have cleansed the atmosphere, it is both visible and awe-inspiring. Its high battlements of white stone reflect the sunlight so brilliantly that it is difficult to tell whether the sun or the Citadel is the source of light.

Much after the event, those who claim to have been witnesses explained that, though it was night, a halo of unusually bright light surrounded the Citadel, preventing them from seeing clearly what they report they saw. From a conflicting melange of stories, these facts emerged. At some point during the midnight hour, two hooded figures appeared at the edge of the tallest parapet and with minimal ceremony eased a large, oblong sack over the wall. Other hooded figures then appeared alongside them. Some hurled stones after the sack. One tossed bouquets of flowers. As in slow motion, the sack, then the stones and the flowers, fell down to the ground beneath the great walls. After a few moments, the sack began to move, and what appeared from a distance to be a person emerged and, with the assistance of others who seemed to have expected this strange arrival, moved out of the line of stones and flowers that continued to fall.

1

INTRODUCTION

Long ago, the lowlanders, as the people are known who live in the areas that stretch out below the Citadel and extend far beyond the horizon, had become accustomed to the vagaries of those who ruled from the Citadel. Even so, those who gathered to trade tales of what they termed the midnight bag sacrifice were unable to agree on its meaning. None of them, though, were greatly troubled by the strange event. There was, they had decided, little purpose to wondering about what they could neither understand nor change. Besides, they had grown used to enduring—enduring the burdens of their work, its unfairness, and its likely permanence. The lowlanders labored in the fields or factories where work is hard, hours are long, and wages are hardly sufficient to provide the shelter and sustenance that enable them to continue in the jobs that dominate their lives.

For countless generations, those in the Citadel have ruled the domain that spreads beyond their mountain and includes the lowlands. The Citadel's current residents govern with greater benevolence than did their ancestors, who overran the lowlanders' country hundreds of years before. Even so, they expect as their due the obedience of the lowlanders, who perform the strenuous physical labor necessary for the Citadel's prosperity. Despite their hard work, the lowlanders are neither invited to participate in the Citadel's ruling Council of Elders, nor allowed a claim to the wealth that they help produce but cannot enjoy. Even the lowlanders' most restrained requests for their fair share of the benefits of their labors are rejected.

Perhaps more clearly than the challengers, the guardians of the Citadel's power understand that any real reform would forever change the mountaintop kingdom. This, of course, they are determined to resist. Those in power understand the need for eternal vigilance, and to this task, involving endless intrigue and deception, they willingly devote their lives. They seem not to recognize the larger burden of their power: a gnawing insecurity—precisely that disquieting unease the acquisition of power was supposed to vanquish.

It should be known, though, that the lowlanders were not always resigned to events beyond their control. Their ancestors mounted pe-

*riodic challenges to the Citadel. Quite a few among the living could
still recall the events of some dozens of years ago and repeated the saga
to all those who would listen.*

*A popular lowlander leader had disappeared under suspicious cir-
cumstances following a secret negotiation session with Citadel officials.
The disappearance, shrouded in secrecy and denial, sparked a great
upheaval among the lowlanders. Many of them spoke out, protested,
and, when all else failed, even took up arms. This group made a strong
and insistent demand for representation at the governing level of the
Citadel. Those who took up the fight did so in the face of great hostility
and very real danger. The Citadel's swift and ruthless retaliation
caused uncounted thousands to suffer economic ruin, or to fear it.
Thousands more endured the perils of arrest and imprisonment at the
hands of lowlander officials in the employ of the Citadel who, viewing
the insurgents as ingrates, subversives, and traitors, treated them accordingly. Even ordinary lowlanders, those who would have benefitted
from a successful revolt, were ambivalent about the wisdom of revolutionary actions that brought down the Citadel's wrath upon them
all. None could deny, though, that the struggle contributed to a sense
of instability in the land—one that even the Citadel's top rulers could
not ignore.*

Four years have passed since I announced on April 24, 1990, that I
would take an unpaid leave from my position on the Harvard Law
School faculty until at least one woman of color was appointed to the
faculty on a permanent basis. Despite the passage of time in a society
where the interest span for even major events is notoriously short, I
continue to receive recognition from groups and organizations, con-
gratulatory letters from strangers, warm greetings from people who
recognize me on the streets, and a measure of respect from real ce-
lebrities I meet at social gatherings. I accept the attention, although
the hope for action and not an expectation of public acclaim
prompted my decision to protest. I accept it although I don't under-

stand it. Lone protesters like myself are more likely to be scorned than commended. Those who challenge the racial status quo, whether it be slavery, segregation, or the current mockery of equal opportunity, are fortunate if they are simply ignored. Honors for even the martyred among them are strictly rationed.

When I decided to take leave from my teaching duties, my intent was to protest Harvard's refusal to hire and tenure a woman of color. Twenty years after hiring me as the school's first full-time black law professor, Harvard's diversity record at the Law School was poor and in the rest of the University appalling. Harvard's claim that it made good-faith efforts to diversify its almost entirely white and male faculty was belied by the fact that not even one Latino, Asian, or Native American professor had joined the law faculty. Although over the years a half-dozen black men gained faculty appointments, Harvard had stood aside while women of color taught and earned tenured positions at other prestigious law schools, including Georgetown, New York University, and the University of Pennsylvania.[1]

My protest reflected my desire to support and further the continuing efforts of students to diversify the faculty. Most recently, those efforts had focused on Harvard's failure to appoint a black woman to the law faculty. I had few expectations that my protest would, by itself, cause Harvard to alter the elitist hiring standards that, for many faculty members, are as close to a religion as they are likely to come. As in my earlier protests at Harvard and elsewhere, however, I hoped that my drastic action might both fortify students and perhaps even prompt a few faculty members to take a stand that would apply sufficient pressure to get Harvard to do for a woman of color in 1990 what they had done for me two decades earlier.

It didn't happen. In retrospect, I see that I placed too little weight on the power of Harvard's prestige and the opportunities that come with a Harvard diploma or professorship. Few are willing to risk losing either. Perhaps I also underestimated the degree to which Harvard faculty would regard the call for diversity as antithetical to the school's mission. Here, I am referring not to the frequent argument that the

Introduction

inclusion of a woman of color would irreparably compromise the rigorous standards of excellence for which Harvard stands. Instead, the faculty's fundamental mission is to preserve Harvard as a place run to protect the faculty's own interests. Since at Harvard, unlike many other law schools, meaningful student involvement in decisions about faculty hiring and promotion is out of the question, most faculty members were not much moved by appeals to add women of color because students in general, and minority women in particular, wanted them hired.

Individual students and faculty members wished me well. Alumni supporters wrote letters. The media coverage was mostly positive. But in the absence of social turmoil like that of the late 1960s which helped persuade Harvard to hire me, my protest and that of the student activists whose efforts I supported were simply inadequate. I extended my protest leave for a second year and requested a third. The University, relying on a rule limiting faculty leaves to two consecutive years—a rule they deemed sufficiently neutral to avoid charges of retaliation—refused my request. My options: either return to my teaching duties or lose my tenured position. Given the school's failure to hire and tenure even one woman of color, I refused to return. And, on June 30, 1992, the University ended my sixteen-year career at the Harvard Law School. Having been the first black professor tenured by Harvard Law School, I became one of the few of any race to be fired.

My protest cost me a tenured position on what many consider the nation's most prestigious law faculty. With my departure, I forfeited the opportunity to teach and perhaps influence hundreds of America's most impressive students. Most distressing to me, despite my protest action, Harvard's hiring and tenure policies continue to give emphasis to paper credentials that, while not guaranteeing excellence, serve to exclude minorities as well as ethnic and working-class whites.[2] Judging from the results, I must conclude that I moved the school's policies in a direction opposite to that I intended.

It is not difficult to assess the costs of my protest. I disappointed

INTRODUCTION

the expectations of students who hoped to take my courses. My voice in faculty debates, while usually unpersuasive, is now silent. Reform-oriented policies that I would have supported have lost my vote. While I have gained many new friends through my protests, I have also lost a significant few. Finally, as I shall discuss in more detail, the overall response to my protest reflects how much easier it is to be misunderstood by your allies than it is to persuade your opponents. It is little wonder that few individuals are willing to stand and challenge unjust practices rather than remain passive and prudently silent.

The commendations I have received, as welcome as they are, have not resolved the need to understand the reasons some persons applaud a protest that so obviously failed to achieve its stated goal. Surely, some expressions of appreciation are motivated by a shared commitment to ending exclusionary patterns in hiring. The applause of others reflects their approval of my stand for women and against mighty Harvard University. In the view of both groups, I had struck an important—albeit, mainly symbolic—blow for civil rights and women's right to receive nondiscriminatory treatment.

Halting the assessment here though would omit the likelihood that, like Martin Luther King, Thurgood Marshall, and many, many others, I am recognized by those who feel comfortable complimenting me only because I have not accomplished my goal. While they may admire the sacrifice I made, they would not agree with and cannot support the ends I sought. The wise protester, then, whose actions are met with applause, should acknowledge its sound while knowing that the cheers are not necessarily a sign of support and may well conceal a discreet opposition.

For me, there were far more pressing reasons than the hope for praise or publicity to risk confrontation. Even so, I want all those who honor individual actions that appear based on a commitment to serve others to know that they offer a value beyond commendation. It is reassurance. For the affliction of all do-good protesters is the knowledge—usually gained in painful ways—that there are no unmitigated good works. Each action intended to help some will unintentionally harm or disadvantage others who, as a result of our well-intended efforts, will feel—and may well be—less well off. While striving to do the Lord's work, we will look to many of our adversaries and some of our friends like the Devil incarnate. All too often, this image survives the gratitude of those who have benefitted from our labors. There is no solution to this, the protester's dilemma. But there is a balm for its pain in the recognition and encouragement from neutral observers who—we must assume—have seen the big picture, have weighed our good intentions against any evils we unleashed, and found us, there is no better word, worthy.

When compared to so many courageous stands by others in heroic causes, my efforts and, yes, even the issues involved in my protest against Harvard, are insignificant. Adding a woman of color to Harvard Law School's faculty will not alter the tragic fact that black people are becoming impoverished, disenfranchised, and incarcerated at alarming rates. Given that admission, I am obligated to examine whether my Harvard protest is not, at best, a meaningless manifestation of personal frustration. At worst, it may have served as a dangerous diversion of public attention from those racial issues most prefer to ignore in the vain hope that a peaceful resolution will burst forth, phoenix-like, from a studied—though increasingly dangerous—neglect.

It is difficult to imagine that one person, acting alone or even with others, will be able with a single blow to eliminate the biggest social challenges of our time. Surely, though, our inability to solve the world's most pressing problems does not mean we should not take on those we can. In this book, I will suggest the value of individual protest actions with all their attendant risks and the slim chance that they will lead to meaningful reform. For one thing, through my years of challenging a host of injustices, I have learned that those in power regard every act of protest—whether against the most mundane rule or the most fundamental principle—as equally threatening. The re-

INTRODUCTION

sistance I experienced at Harvard was as determined as that I have encountered at any institution that is satisfied with the status quo and fearful of change. By challenging authority, the protester undermines the assumption that things are either as they are supposed to be or as they must be. What is most heretical, though, is that, in every case, the protester asserts the right to have a meaningful—as opposed to a token—voice. That is what those in authority resist so desperately.

ONE

Models for Confrontation

*A*t the time of what is remembered as the Great Revolt, Xercis was Protector of the Citadel, its top leader. At that time, he had only recently inherited his position from his father in a line of succession that stretched back beyond the memory of any now living. From birth, he had been trained for the position he had held for three decades with a dedication that knew no limit. Indeed, Xercis tended the Citadel's great traditions with all the fierce devotion of a high priest in some ancient temple. Even his detractors acknowledged that his stewardship was without parallel.

Xercis had considered his father's rule overly harsh, condemning the lowlanders to virtual serfdom. Accordingly, soon after he was named Protector, he eased the most onerous taxes his father had levied upon the lowlanders working in factories and on small farms. But with the current unrest, he had to concede that his well-intended actions were a mistake. Thoroughly downtrodden peoples exhaust themselves with the tasks of survival. It is when their conditions improve, however slightly, that some among them envision a better life and, nurturing dreams of freedom, sow the seeds of eventual revolt.

Even now, the lowlanders were resenting and resisting laws promulgated by the Citadel that were humane by comparison with those issued at earlier times. This unrest, slight as it still was, worried the Citadel's leaders. They would have worried even more had they known

9

CONFRONTING AUTHORITY

that there dwelt within the Citadel, within their Protector's very household, one who was sympathetic to the lowlanders. This was Tamar, Xercis' daughter and only child. Tamar's mother had died in childbirth. Xercis had devoted himself to Tamar's education. She had a keen mind, and at an early age exhibited a remarkable grasp of the complex doctrines and arcane language of the Citadel's government. He gave her both his wide knowledge and a strong independence of mind. He was proud of the first, but came to be ambivalent about the second.

Tamar viewed the protesting lowlanders with a fresh eye. She had worked with them in their hospitals and taught in their schools. She believed that they should not be put down as traitors; rather that they should be treated as equals. Xercis' early difficulties with reform occurred, she believed, because his reforms had not gone far enough. But Tamar was devoted to her father and for a long time kept her ideas to herself. Then, the Citadel's harsh reaction to the early stages of the lowlanders' current protests moved her to speak out.

"Are their demands," she finally burst out, "so unreasonable? Their labor and their skills are the source of the Citadel's wealth, its strength. Is it fair—is it wise—to deny them a voice in what their labor makes possible?"

Xercis was speechless. Maintaining power was the Citadel's central duty. Could it be that Tamar, while having the intellect, skill, and courage to rule, lacked the devotion to authority and tradition so vital to the Citadel's effective governance? For the future, a barrier loomed, one that threatened a quiet transition of power when Xercis died or stepped down.

Whenever I am asked about the source of my willingness to challenge authority, I respond with a story about my mother and the landlord. It was in the mid-1930s, during the Great Depression. My family lived in the Hill, the mainly black area of Pittsburgh, Pennsylvania. I was six or seven years old, but I remember my mother, Ada Childress

Bell, taking my brother, Charles, and me with her to the rent office. My mother, standing in front of the barred teller's window, taking cash from her purse, waved it in front of the clerk. That is all I really remember, but I learned later that she told him, "This is the rent money. I have it—and you will get it when you fix the back steps so that my children won't fall and hurt themselves." Then, we left the office.

It was not until many years later that I recognized my mother's strength. She was willing to face eviction in order to gain a safe habitation, the right to which was not then recognized by the law and would not be for decades. In those economically dreary times, my father worked as a laborer whenever he could find a job. We had no savings, and had the landlord evicted us for nonpayment of rent, we really would have had no place to go. "What happened?" I asked. My mother, even many years later, beamed. "They fixed the steps," she said proudly. "And," she added, "they fixed all the steps along the row of houses where we lived." Even more years later, I asked her, "Did your neighbors know what you did?" "Not from me, they didn't," she replied, and then, noting my surprise, answered the question I would have asked. "Many of those people were friends. I didn't want them to feel beholden to me for something I did for my family, something," she added, "I did for myself."

Her story gave me a keen insight into the subtleties of confronting those in authority. My mother also used the direct approach in dealing with our schoolteachers. At even a hint of a problem, she was at the school speaking quietly and firmly as she got at the issue and helped work out a solution. I think our school's awareness that she would come there on short notice served to alleviate a good many small problems before they became big ones.

My father, Derrick Bell, Sr., served as a different, but no less important, role model. He worked hard to provide his family with food, shelter, and clothing. It was a matter of pride with him that my mother did not hold a job and was available to her children full-time.

CONFRONTING AUTHORITY

He did not, as far as I knew, confront his white bosses directly. He had been born in Dothan, Alabama, and came to Pittsburgh in the late 1920s with a sixth-grade education. He seldom talked about the South and never returned there until quite late in his life. But around whites he exuded a quiet strength in his conduct that was almost tangible.

My father died in 1970. Late in his life, he told my sister Janet of having been beaten as a youngster by three white boys. As he told it, he had worked hard picking cotton to earn money to take his girlfriend to the county fair. His mother let him wear his good white shirt. At the fair, he won a small toy whip and was snapping it to the amusement of his girlfriend. The three white youths, each armed with a real whip, took exception to what they considered "a nigger playing at being a white man." They whipped my father with their whips until he was so bloody that his girlfriend had to lead him home. The police were called, and because my grandfather was a well-known minister, they took them both in a police buggy around town looking for the youths. They did not find them. Later, though, my father reported that he came across two of the young whites on a deserted road—and without their whips. He beat up both of them.

We all celebrated when, in the mid-1930s, my father obtained a porter's job in Kaufmann's, one of Pittsburgh's largest department stores. He kept his floor clean and received a regular salary plus discounts on purchases. The work was hard, but relatively clean, and there was no heavy lifting and less of the abuse that came with work in laboring gangs. In those pre-state-lottery times, a great many people in the black community and—as I later learned—quite a few whites played "the numbers." It involved daily bets on a three-digit number or its components selected from the daily stock exchange total or some other agreed-on, published figure. Those who guessed correctly were said to have "hit" the numbers and were paid at the rate of seven hundred to one.

Models for Confrontation

In addition to his duties as a floor porter at the department store, my father picked up the numbers played by the maids, porters, and salespeople on his floor and turned them into a "banker" who paid off those who won and other employees, pocketing the rest. This provided additional income, and when, about 1939, my father "hit" the numbers for a dollar, thereby winning about $700, my mother convinced him to place his winnings on the down payment for a three-bedroom, brick house in a nicer neighborhood. It was on one of the higher hills in Pittsburgh with a park across the street and beautiful views of the city through our back windows. The schools were better and our mainly white neighbors were friendly, though they tended to move away as soon as their daughters reached puberty.

When, after several years, my father developed narcolepsy and doctors advised that, along with medication, outdoor work would help him stay awake, he left his porter job—he had given up the numbers after a rather disastrous effort to "book" them (cover the numbers bets himself)—and started a refuse hauling business. Beginning with an old, rented truck, over the years he obtained contracts with major stores and office buildings. My brother and I, teenagers by that time, would sometimes work with him on one of the two or three large trucks he acquired. At the loading platforms, the white supervisors would joke with the black men who worked for my father, exchanging jokes, punching them lightly on the arm. But it was as if my father was surrounded by an invisible shield that they knew better than to invade. He was all business. Although he called them "Mister," and they usually called him "Al," his nickname, there was a respect in their dealings with him, a no-nonsense aspect to their conversations that served to close the status differences created by custom and enforced by the whites' dominance in racial relationships.

My family enjoyed what was, by black folks' standards, a middle-class life. My parents encouraged and paid for my college education and that of my brother and two sisters. Even so, my father never forgot and tried to pass on what he had learned about race during a hard life. I remember, for example, living in my parents' home while attending law school after returning from two years in the military. One of my white classmates had stopped by to give me some papers. We visited for a short time and after he left, my father, who had come home during the friend's visit, told me, "Son, this is your house and if you want to invite white people here, you are welcome to do so. But, as for me, I never trusted them." It struck me then that, except for the insurance man or repair people, no whites entered our house, certainly not for a social occasion.

Neither of my parents hated whites. They simply dealt realistically with race issues as they found them. My father often cited from a mental collection of racial assertions. Example: "Son, you must work hard because white folks are planning and scheming while we Negroes are eating and sleeping." His way of illustrating the rarity or extra-fine quality of some object was to state that "very few whites and no Negroes own a car like that." My mother, for her part, would often claim that when shopping, if she saw a group of whites gathered around a counter, she would plow right in, assuming that if whites were buying an item it was something she should at least peruse. And yes, like so many black parents, mine frequently warned my siblings and me that because we were black, we would have to be twice as good to get half as much as whites.

Because of my parents' hard work and sacrifices for the family, I have been able to live in a much broader world than they knew. My relationships with whites as peers, as friends, as supervisors and employees have been more positive than my father's. And yet, divisions along racial lines are so deep, so set, that there have been more than a few occasions in my life when I have remembered my father's distrust of whites and wished that I had heeded his warning.

My parents were wonderful role models, but they were not the sole sources of the confidence that contributed to whatever assurance it takes to confront authorities. I owe a great deal to my extended family. Uncles, aunts, and older cousins, all of whom encouraged my many activities, applauded my achievements, and provided me with stamp collector albums, a photographic darkroom, tape recorders, or whatever a current hobby or interest might require.

Another strong influence was the black church. My mother attended church regularly and my father from time to time—though almost never after he developed narcolepsy. In my youth, we attended an African Methodist Episcopal church (AME), and after we purchased a home, transferred to a nearby, all-black Presbyterian church whose longtime minister, Rev. Harold Tolliver, was a good man, a virtual model of godliness. The church and the manse were on my paper route, and Rev. Tolliver and his wife did their share to convince me that I was something special.

The newspaper route that I kept all through junior and senior high school gave me the satisfaction of earning my own spending money. Because of housing segregation—mandated by policy and custom rather than law, but no less rigidly enforced—my mostly black customers ranged across the social and economic spectrum from welfare recipients to laborers and post office employees, to a doctor, a few ministers, small businessmen, lawyers, and the one black judge in our area, Judge Homer S. Brown. The black professionals on my route all lived in close proximity with working-class people. Their homes were nicer and they provided a great deal of stability to the neighborhood that was lost in later years when they or their children were able to move out to formerly all-white areas.

I decided to go to law school because of the kindness and encouragement I received from many of my newspaper customers. Judge Brown and his wife, Billie, and Judge Brown's next-door neighbors, lawyer Everett Utterback and his wife, Bernice, virtually adopted me. They invited me in for tea, to visit on holidays, and were always ready with advice that in short let me know that "we made it and so can you." The one black city councilman, Paul Jones, was also supportive. He spoke at my high school and took me aside afterward for a long talk about the benefits of becoming a lawyer. Each of these individuals and several others whose names I can no longer remember took an interest in my school progress and spoke favorably about going on to college. I appreciated their encouragement and, I must admit, was favorably impressed by their affluence, which both ensured that they were able to pay for their papers each week, and seemed, as well, to provide them with a worldliness that I envied and longed to emulate. All were models for me.

When I returned to Pittsburgh to begin law school after two years in the military, I discovered that I was the only black in my class of one hundred and forty students. There were no women in the law school and only one or two blacks in other classes. One of them, K. Leroy Irvis, had just graduated after doing extremely well in his classes and serving on the law review. An older man, Irvis and his wife, Catherine, took me under their wings and literally taught me the ropes about legal education. Irvis gave me valuable insights into my teachers, in addition to good advice on study habits, note-taking, and exam preparation. He warned that my first-year property teacher was from Mississippi and, while a good and friendly man, at some point during the course he would tell a story about a Negro sneaking late at night into a watermelon patch—all to make a point about the laws of trespass and adverse possession. Irvis—a quite militant black man who later became the first black speaker of the House of Representatives in the state legislature—urged me not to protest but simply to sit there quietly.[1] The professor did tell the story and I followed Irvis's advice. I earned a good grade in property. Today, I would not be able to remain silent in the face of such a story, regardless of the cost, but the truth is that there have been countless times when—for one reason or another—I failed to challenge a racial statement I found demeaning, insulting, or in bad taste.

After doing well in my first year of law school, I was elected to the law review and managed to write a record number of articles—virtually all of them on civil rights subjects. During those years, I learned about black lawyers who had made major civil rights contributions:

Models for Confrontation

Charles Houston, the first black legal counsel for the NAACP, his successor Thurgood Marshall, and the first black federal judge, William H. Hastie, himself an accomplished civil rights lawyer. These men were inspirations, but I had no hope of equaling their work. After all, the Supreme Court had struck down state-endorsed segregation in 1954, the year I entered law school. And no less an eminence than Judge Hastie told me when I travelled to Philadelphia to meet him during my final year of law school, that while my interest in civil rights was praiseworthy, I was born fifteen years too late to make it a career.

Judge Hastie's view was shared by a great many people back in 1957. I had no reason to disagree. The disappointment of my expectation that racism would end has certainly fueled some of my protests, and may have inspired them all. Thus, as important as they were, I can't honestly say that the inspiration and encouragement of family and friends were the sole influences shaping my resolve. They had gained what status they had by learning to play within the system. It seemed to me as the 1960s dawned with precious little real racial reform, that the benefits of compliance were slim, and the need for confrontation was ever more apparent.

It was in this spirit that I decided to resign from my first lawyering job rather than give up my two-dollar NAACP membership, which my supervisors at the U.S. Department of Justice deemed a conflict of interest. I had obtained the Justice Department position after a few faculty members at the University of Pittsburgh Law School noticed as graduation approached that, despite quite good grades and a law review editorship, I had no job offers. The one large Pittsburgh law firm that invited the top students in my class for interviews was candid: they were, I was told, not ready to hire a black associate. William Rogers, then the Deputy Attorney General, presented the speech at our law review banquet and, evidently having been apprised of my plight, urged me to apply to the Justice Department's honor graduate recruitment program. I did and was hired.

Faced with the order to give up my NAACP membership, I consulted a number of successful blacks I knew. Almost unanimously they urged me to remain at the Justice Department and work from within. They pointed out that I had been in the newly formed Civil Rights Division for only several months, and its leaders were still finding their way in a politically sensitive area. It was comforting counsel, particularly since I had no other job prospects. I received somewhat different advice from Judge Hastie. As I recall, Hastie, like the others, pointed out that there were no more than a handful of black lawyers in the federal government and only two black lawyers in the new Civil Rights Division. In the end, Hastie emphasized that I should do what I felt was right. He did not mention it, but his own life gave meaning to what he viewed as right.

In 1941, Hastie had accepted a position as civilian aide to the Secretary of War—one of the highest posts held by a black person in the federal government at that time. Hastie had doubts about accepting this position. He worried that he would be used to legitimize the segregation of black soldiers but relented after Justice Felix Frankfurter reportedly assured him that he would be able to work from within to improve conditions for Negro soldiers.[2] At the time of Hastie's appointment, it was the policy of the armed services to segregate Negro soldiers in separate, and certainly unequal, units. Although he knew that military leaders were not prepared to accept integration, Hastie made it clear that he would settle for nothing less.[3] He soon found, however, that he could not achieve more than minor changes in military practices that subjected black soldiers to a steady barrage of racial epithets and violence, more severe punishment, and inferior facilities. Disheartened, and realizing that he could neither end segregation in the military nor make even the less significant reforms for which he fought as determinedly, Hastie resigned in 1943. Believing that only public pressure would change these policies, Hastie felt he would be more useful as a private citizen. On a personal level, he could no longer abide what he thought was a deliberate campaign by those around him to undermine his work and break his will.[4]

Models for Confrontation

Hastie's departure was lauded in the black press.[5] W. E. B. Du Bois's comments both commended Hastie and defined a standard of public service that remains more the exception than the norm.

> There are two sorts of public relations officials in Washington working on the situation of the Negro: one sort is a kind of upper clerk who transmits to the public with such apologetic airs as he can assume, the refusal of the department to follow his advice or the advice of anyone else calculated to cease the racial situation. The other kind of race relations official seeks to give advice and to get the facts and if he receives a reasonable amount of cooperation he works on hopeful. If he does not, he withdraws. It is, of course, this second type of official alone who is useful and valuable. The other is nothing. Hastie belongs to the valuable sort and will not be easily replaced.[6]

The Defense Department, with attention upon it and the loss of a visible symbol of its commitment, was forced to make changes. Personnel was changed, equal opportunity for the races was finally acknowledged as a goal, and some efforts were made to improve the morale of African American soldiers—all reforms that Hastie had advocated. Finally, in 1948, President Truman signed Executive Order 9981, abolishing segregation in the armed forces.[7] As for Hastie, he went on to become governor of the Virgin Islands and eventually a federal judge.

With Hastie's protest in mind, I decided not to give up my NAACP membership, reported my refusal to my superiors, and waited to be fired or transferred. Justice Department officials did neither. Rather, I was moved to a desk set up in the hall. I was barred from doing any race-related work and instead was given a series of non-race-related research projects. It was busy work. I took the hint and resigned.

Like Hastie, good fortune has always followed my protest actions—which is one reason I have been able to continue them. Thus, when I left the Justice Department, I returned home to Pittsburgh early in 1959, where Marian Jordan, one of my former newspaper customers, recommended me as her replacement as the executive director of the Pittsburgh branch of the NAACP. I accepted the job and gained an understanding—much of it the hard way—of the administrative and fund-raising aspects of civil rights work which lawyers seldom experience. The branch had little money either for my salary or for the work we needed to do, and there were many frustrations and setbacks. But my job allowed me to practice the confrontational approach I so admired in others.

In 1959, many public facilities in Pittsburgh remained segregated. I organized groups to "test" these facilities. It was relatively easy to recruit volunteers for excursions to the white swimming pool in the county-run park, or the white skating rink in a neighboring town. It was harder to get the volunteers to actually show up. I never shall forget the evening I walked into a downtown bar that did not serve blacks. Several black friends had promised to join me there. None did. As I sat at the bar, some of the white patrons began muttering about the stranger. I heard sotto-voiced calls to "throw the nigger out" and worse. No one said anything to me, including the bartender, who ignored my repeated order for a beer. Finally, discretion gained the upper hand over whatever valor I had been able to muster. I walked out. When the civil rights sit-ins began on a national scale the following year, my respect for their courage was based firmly on my experience.

After several months in the Pittsburgh job, Thurgood Marshall, then Director Counsel of the NAACP Legal Defense and Educational Fund (LDF), came to town for a speech. He asked me, "What's a lawyer like you doing working in a non-lawyer job?" I began to explain, but in his usual gruff way, Marshall cut me off. "Why don't you come on up to New York and work with me?" I accepted on the spot. Many years later, Marshall told me that he had hired me at the urging of his good friend, Judge William Hastie, who had told Marshall of my Justice Department experience.

Had I suppressed my feeling that the required surrender of my NAACP membership was wrong, I might have toiled on, unhappily,

Models for Confrontation

at the Justice Department for years at work less risky but certainly no less frustrating than my job with the Pittsburgh NAACP. More important, had I remained at the Justice Department, I would have missed the chance to work with the NAACP Legal Defense Fund during some of the most exciting years of the civil rights movement.

In January 1960 when I arrived in New York, there were, including me, only five lawyers on the LDF staff: Thurgood Marshall, Jack Greenberg, Constance Baker Motley, and James Nabrit. Robert L. Carter, Thurgood's long-time assistant, had assumed the general counsel's position at the NAACP when that organization split off from LDF for tax and other reasons. Marshall assigned me to work with Carter, who became my friend and mentor. Carter, a brilliant lawyer and a tough taskmaster, taught me that a black man could stand up to either a hostile Southern judge or an arrogant waiter in a fine restaurant and not only survive, but gain results and a measure of respect. Indeed, Carter resigned as the NAACP's General Counsel in 1968—and the rest of his legal staff followed him—after the organization's board of directors refused to provide a hearing to one of Carter's staff lawyers, Lewis Steel, whom the Board had summarily dismissed after he published an article critical of the U.S. Supreme Court.[8] Quite clearly, if I had to point to one model for my confrontational tendencies, it would be Robert L. Carter.

Then and now, a major inspiration for my protest activity came from my contact as an LDF lawyer with Southern blacks who challenged segregation either by becoming named plaintiffs in civil rights suits or by participating in direct action protests—sometimes both. In their no-nonsense, matter-of-fact courage and commitment they seemed to be determined to confront those who had kept blacks down for so long, rather than harboring any real hope that whites would ever change. Staying in their homes—sometimes with volunteer guards stationed at the windows at night—escorting them to court, sitting in on their planning meetings, one sensed their feelings of triumph even though their cases were later lost. For them, finding the courage to challenge the fixed-in-stone racial system was itself a significant victory, whatever the outcome of the court case.

Dick Gregory tells a story that illustrates the quiet dignity with which these brave black people confronted segregation—a dignity that I could only admire. In an auditorium in Jackson, Mississippi, Gregory heard an old man give a speech about how he had been involved in a voter registration campaign and had been jailed for killing a man sent to burn his house in reprisal. "I didn't mind going to jail for freedom, no I wouldn't even mind being killed for freedom. But my wife and I was married for a long time, and, well, you know I ain't never spent a night away from home. While I was in jail, my wife died."[9]

Gregory recalls how he felt listening to this old man:

> That destroyed me . . . [T]his man bucked and rose up and fought the system for me, and he went to jail for me, and he lost his wife for me. He had gone out on the battle lines and demonstrated for a tomorrow he wouldn't ever see, for jobs and rights he might not even be qualified to benefit from. A little old man from a country town who never spent a night away from his wife in his married life. And he went to jail for me and being away killed her.[10]

Such poignant stories about what our black clients had to deal with every day made us civil rights lawyers uneasy when people lauded us for showing up at hostile courts and facing hostile local citizens and law enforcement officials. Thurgood Marshall expressed this discomfort when journalist Carl Rowan made the mistake of praising him for his courage: "You forget just one little fucking thing. I go into these places and I come out, on the fastest vehicle moving. The brave blacks are the ones who have to live there after I leave."[11]

Harry Briggs's experience was far too typical. Briggs was the first plaintiff in a lawsuit Thurgood Marshall filed in 1950 against a school board in Clarendon County, South Carolina, challenging the segre-

Models for Confrontation

gated school system. Pressured by the county's white leaders to with-draw the suit, Briggs refused to relent. Thereafter, he was fired from his job pumping gas. The White Citizens' Council stopped all deliveries of food, drinks, and laundry to the motel where his wife, Eliza, worked. When their boycott achieved its goal, persuading its owners to fire her, the Briggs turned to farming, but found that no one would give them credit or sell them supplies.[12] Although Harry Briggs's suit—the first legal attack on segregation in elementary schools—was lost at the trial level, he felt proud of his efforts when he watched Marshall argue their case in court.[13] The case was consolidated with *Brown v. Board of Education* before the Supreme Court, where Briggs's suffering was finally rewarded.[14]

The slight chance that the law would vindicate trampled-on rights cannot explain how some blacks, born and reared under a system committed to their subordination, found the courage to confront powerful whites for whom no retaliatory action was too dastardly. I think there must also have been a measure of pure rage that manifests itself in a determination to harass the system—even at considerable personal risk—using civil rights activity as the weapon.

An incident in my own experience that tapped this rage occurred in the 1960s. One bitterly cold winter night, I was flying across the South, headed for Jackson, Mississippi, when a blizzard forced the plane down in Memphis, Tennessee. Passengers were told to line up to get hotel reservations. I don't remember where the white passengers were assigned, but I was told to go to a black motel, the Lorraine, later to gain unhappy fame as the place where Dr. Martin Luther King was killed. It was late when the airport bus dropped me there. The sleepy clerk assigned me to a room that had not been cleaned since its apparent earlier use by some of the motel's "transient trade," but I decided to make the best of it. Unfortunately, the room was also unheated. After an hour or so of discomfort, I decided to take one of the other options offered at the airport—a late train to Jackson.

Arriving in that city cold and tired, after an uncomfortable several hours on the crowded, unheated train, I went into the waiting room to call Jack Young, one of only three black lawyers in the state, to ask him to pick me up. Before I could place the call, two very large, white policemen banged on the booth and ordered me out. Only then did I realize that I was in the white waiting room. Nonetheless, my anger overcoming appropriate prudence, I explained why I was using the phone and tried to complete my call. The policemen paid no attention, continuing to order me out. They dragged me out of the telephone booth and placed me under arrest. I spent the rest of the night in jail. On the way to what I hoped was the station, I realized that my rage had placed me in a vulnerable position. I was fearful for my safety, but proud of my rage. I imagine any number of civil rights activists have experienced quite similar feelings.

When I left the Legal Defense Fund in 1966 to accept a position as Deputy Director of Civil Rights at the old Department of Health, Education, and Welfare, I found that the people there were as resistant to reform as so many of the recalcitrant federal judges I encountered in the South had been. In government, judicial hostility was replaced by political prudence so extreme that it verged on irresponsibility. Peter Libassi, the Department's Director of Civil Rights, frequently felt the weight of my frustration. Libassi was actually a quite effective administrator, but in my view he took far too long to take action against local school districts which were continuing to receive federal financial assistance despite their refusal to desegregate their schools.

I constantly reminded Libassi that our job under the law (Title VI of the Civil Rights Act of 1964) was to cut off funds to slow-moving school boards and other entities that continued racially discriminatory policies. Often, we would take all of the elaborate preparatory steps, but still Libassi delayed. On a few occasions, with the aid and encouragement of Ruby Martin, the third person in line in the office and later Virginia's Secretary of Administration, we sent cases on to Congress for action when Peter was out of town. My second stint with the federal government was better than the first, but again it was frustrating to watch racial issues receiving back burner priority.

"Are you having fun?" a government colleague of those days was fond of asking me as we rode back from a meeting at the White House or gathered for a session with members of Congress on Capitol Hill. He viewed civil rights policy-making as a giant chess game with exciting players and challenging obstacles. "No," I would always respond. I knew how many black people across the South were looking to us to desegregate their schools and health facilities. Even modest programs were painfully hard to design, easily sidetracked and, once delayed, hard to get started again. I thought of Judge Hastie and his frustrating stint in the War Department. Unlike those in the military who undermined his efforts, those with whom I worked were trying to do a good job. Against serious political obstacles, they were working from within. Whether because of my background, my experiences working in the South, or the examples of those who were my models, I found my work neither satisfying nor very productive. It was, I knew, time to look for another job.

TWO

A Reason for Protest

*X*ercis *and Tamar had many heated arguments about the Citadel's treatment of the lowlanders. "You are young and headstrong, Tamar," Xercis told her. "Reserve your conclusions until you are older and have more experience. Our treatment of the lowlanders is firm but not brutal, rigid but not inappropriate."*

"Much as I respect your wisdom, father," she responded, "it does not moderate the Citadel's harsh rules. It does not relieve the lowlanders. Real reform is needed. And without it," she paused, "turmoil is inevitable."

"Tamar," Xercis spoke sternly, "the price of maintaining power over others is the continuing risk of their revolt. But we must abide by the teaching of our forebears. Whatever its cost, we must maintain dominance. An alternative to our power, gained through revolt, might well beget less justice rather than more." Tamar opened her mouth to respond, but Xercis would not be interrupted. "Because of your work among the lowlanders, my daughter, you have changed. No longer the missionary from the Citadel to them, you are increasingly their advocate against the Citadel."

Tamar was moved by the deep hurt and frustration in her father's voice. "I am a missionary for all, seeking rights and justice for all," she responded quietly. Xercis looked at his daughter and slowly shook his head. "Those are only words, my child. Your quest for the unreal

27

imperils your chance to become the Citadel's first woman Protector. In this position, you would see more clearly the limits as well as the potential of your crusades."

"But father . . ." Xercis interrupted, unable to bear her attitude. He spoke with finality. "You, Tamar, must decide whether you will carry on the traditions of our hallowed forebears or those of a race who were their traditional enemies. But Tamar, know, as you weigh your decision, that the Citadel is and must remain opposed to granting equality to the lowlanders."

Friends and family have both raised the question: even with all my frustrations, why protest what I viewed as the Harvard Law School's shortcomings by taking a leave without pay? There were any number of ways to express my disagreement with the faculty's failure to do immediately what it surely would do eventually: hire and tenure a woman of color. And yet, I was considering a protest that would cut off my major source of income and, in all likelihood, eventually jeopardize my position. I held a chair, the Weld Professorship. The Law School's prestige provided a highly visible platform for my writings and other professional activities. Tenure ensured that my frequent differences with school authorities and my not infrequent public protests against school policy would not place my job in jeopardy.

"And," family and friends added: "your life at Harvard, while hardly idyllic, is far from unbearable." They were right. My faculty colleagues and I came from different worlds, held disparate views on most issues, and yet I had cordial relationships with all of them, and a goodly number of friendships. And why not? Our divergent approaches to teaching and scholarship aside, we were engaged in the same enterprise. None of us liked grading final exams or attending faculty meetings. But beyond the grousing about the down-side of our work, most felt that teaching law in general—and teaching at Harvard, in particular—was the best job in the world. One of my faculty friends, Professor Frank Michelman, advised, "Don't listen to their grumbling. You couldn't pour most of these guys out of here."

In effect, those who cared about my welfare, like those who years before had urged me to drop my NAACP membership and continue working for civil rights within the Justice Department, were suggesting that my position at Harvard was unique and should not be jeopardized. My advisors were right about the uniqueness of my position, but it was precisely the unique character of my role that necessitated my protest. My effectiveness as a "first black" depended on never letting the Law School forget the nature of my appointment and the commitments we both made at that time.

A Faculty Appointment as Mission

When in the Spring of 1969 I accepted the Harvard Law School's offer to join its faculty, both the school and I had reason to recognize that mine was a pioneering appointment, a mission really, that would mark a turning point in the school's history. The break in tradition was twofold. First, I would become the first full-time black law teacher in Harvard's one-hundred-fifty-year history. Second, unlike virtually all the faculty at that time, my qualifications did not include either graduation with distinction from a prestigious law school or a judicial clerkship on the Supreme Court. I had not, moreover, practiced with a major law firm where a well-known partner, himself a Harvard alumnus, was urging my appointment. Thus, my appointment at Harvard breached two hiring rules: one implicit regarding race, and one explicit regarding credentials and connections.

In the late 1960s, I applied for teaching positions at a half dozen law schools, including Harvard, none of which expressed any interest in hiring me. I gave a lecture at Harvard at the invitation of Professor Charles Nesson. I had met him a few years earlier when he was monitoring civil rights trials as a special assistant at the Justice Department. On more than one occasion, he sat in the courtroom as I argued civil rights case appeals. I enjoyed the chance to share my views on racial discrimination, developed over eight or nine years of civil rights experience, with the students in his civil rights class, and they seemed pleased that I was there. But Nesson later reported that school officials told him there was no faculty position for someone with my expertise.

At the least, Nesson got back in touch with me. A meeting with faculty at George Washington Law School set up by a former law school peer, and then a professor there, led nowhere. Not only did I not get a job offer, I never heard from them again. The same thing happened at Michigan Law School. I was speaking on campus and a friend arranged for me to give a talk at a law faculty lunch. Again, everyone was courteous and, though they knew I was interested in a teaching position, no one—including the friend who suggested my name—ever got back in touch with me. I learned later that the snubs were not racial, but simply the dismissive manner in which law faculties deal with candidates in whom they are not interested.

In addition to race, a major barrier was credentials. Law faculties, then and now, were far more interested in where I went to school than anything I had done since. Touro Law School's Dean Howard Glickstein recalls his all too typical experience seeking a law teaching job. He reports:

> It was eighteen years since I had graduated from law school. During these years, I had worked for a leading New York City law firm, and for the Civil Rights Division of the United States Department of Justice, where I argued cases in the federal district and appellate courts, prepared briefs for the Supreme Court and helped draft major legislation. I had also been the General Counsel of a federal agency (United States Commission on Civil Rights) and served in a position to which I was appointed by the President of the United States and confirmed by the United States Senate. Now, I was applying for my first job as a law school faculty member. I was in the presence of a law school dean

who was reviewing my resume. After a few minutes of reading, he looked up, smiled and said, "Oh, I am glad to see that you were on the Yale Law Journal."[1]

My friend and mentor, Judge Robert L. Carter, now on Senior Status in the Southern District of New York, tells a similar but far more shocking story. In 1968, after two decades with the NAACP, during which Carter had won more than two dozen cases in the Supreme Court, including some of the most pathbreaking decisions of the era,[2] he resigned and considered teaching law. The faculty at the Michigan Law School expressed interest. A faculty member called Carter to check his credentials. He noted—without much enthusiasm—that Carter had graduated from the Howard Law School. Then, brightening, he sought confirmation that Carter had obtained an L.L.M. at Columbia. "Great, Mr. Carter. Columbia is a good school. Would you mind very much if we took a look at the grades you earned there?" While Carter expressed no opposition, he did not receive a job offer. Dean Glickstein, Judge Carter, and Lord only knows how many other applicants were rejected despite sterling records of practice because they lacked the law school credentials that, as time proved in these cases, were only poor predictors of future performance.[3]

My introduction to law school teaching was via the back door. Professor Martin Levine, a University of Southern California faculty member responsible for setting up the Western Center on Law and Poverty at USC's Law Center in Los Angeles, offered me the directorship of the Center. I accepted when, in response to my expressed interest in teaching, he added an adjunct professorship to his offer. I didn't realize until later that the impressive-sounding title described a part-time position in which I taught one civil rights course. Even so, it was a good experience. My teaching was barely adequate, but one student told me later, "You were very serious about it." In addition, I was able to see firsthand how law teachers lived. They work hard but their hours are flexible and they have the opportunity to teach and write on whatever interests them. "What a great job," I exclaimed to a group of USC law professors after we had finished a long lunch. I was headed back to my administrative duties at the Western Center's offices. They, on a spur-of-the-moment decision, were off to see an exhibit at a nearby museum. "Now," I observed wryly, "I know why you white guys have been keeping law teaching jobs to yourselves all these years."

I had been at work at the Western Center for only a few months when Dr. Martin Luther King, Jr., was killed in Memphis. As Jewel, still back in Washington, D.C., with our three young children, reported the ominous clouds of black smoke rising from the riots in the heart of the city, I worried about their safety as I grieved the nation's loss. Dr. King, as evidenced by the Poor People's March on Washington that was still in the planning stages at his death, was one of the few leaders who realized that racism is a by-product of the disparities in wealth and opportunity that disadvantage whites as well as blacks.[4] That message, subsequently subsumed in the Vietnam War, has not resurfaced, because our leaders who support social reform underestimate the direct connection between racism and our failure to provide decent jobs, schooling, housing, and health care for an ever-growing percentage of our people, regardless of race.

The message that most policy-makers gained from King's death and the urban insurrections that followed it was that there had been too little change in patterns of employment and education. Major institutions across the country initiated programs intended to alter the status of staffs and work forces that had remained all-white, notwithstanding the Supreme Court's 1954 decision invalidating racial segregation in public schools[5] and the 1964 Civil Rights Act barring discrimination in employment. By early 1968, many of the nation's leading law schools, responding to both the national crisis and student pressures, were beginning to consider hiring one or two blacks for their faculties. Prior to that time, no more than a dozen blacks had ever held full-time faculty positions at white law schools.[6]

A Reason for Protest

The changes that followed were neither voluntary nor significant. In order to stave off more substantial changes, those in power hired a few token qualified blacks—who today remain in largely the same positions in largely the same numbers. The jobs that were set aside for minorities, while better than previous opportunities, never offered the new insiders any real power with which to generate deeper changes in the status quo. Yet, to almost everyone, these surface changes seemed sufficient.[7]

The beneficiaries of policies soon labeled "affirmative action" were seldom those blacks who had taken to the streets.[8] Spurred by a new sense of crisis, institutions began recruiting minorities with training and skills previously deemed "inadequate." Far fewer places were available for the unskilled or unemployed blacks, those who felt the deepest despair. Major law schools, often pressured both by events and by their slightly increased ranks of black students, joined in this tardy recognition that their self-interest would be served by adding one or two blacks to their all-white faculties.

It was early in 1969 that I began receiving expressions of serious interest from several schools, including Harvard. Professor Alan Dershowitz, now a fierce opponent of affirmative action, but then a spirited supporter of black law students, argued that the presence of some blacks in places of prestige would diffuse tensions in black ghettoes. The connection between the ghetto threat and the middle-class remedy was more than a little remote, but black law students did their part to link their desire for black faculty members with the school's readiness to do something. Thus, when for the third time I sought a teaching position at Harvard—this time at the Law School's invitation—faculty members were both friendly and receptive to the possibility that I would join their ranks. The focus was on my potential contributions. No one mentioned, at least within my hearing, that my credentials did not meet all the criteria that so many deemed essential prerequisites.

At Harvard, students do not serve on the committee responsible for reviewing applicants for teaching positions and making recommendations to the full faculty. In my case, though, student approval was quite important. During my visit, I was asked to present a lecture to the black student group. My talk emphasized my civil rights background and my activist approach (for a lawyer) to racial reform. Students who met with the dean and a few senior faculty members strongly urged the appointment of a black teacher and indicated—after my visit—that I was acceptable to them. The faculty subsequently voted me an offer which the then dean, Derek Bok, flew to Los Angeles to deliver to me in person. To help persuade me to accept Harvard's offer, Dean Bok brought with him a representative of the Black Law Students Association (BLSA), Robert Bell (now a judge on Maryland's State Court of Appeals).

During lengthy discussions with Dean Bok, I told him that I viewed teaching as an opportunity to continue my civil rights work in a new arena. When I accepted, I tried to make it clear that I did not wish to be a token black and expected that the school would actively seek and hire other minority lawyers for the faculty. While we did not discuss my previous protest activity, I assumed that everyone was aware of it. In any event, I was satisfied with the school's commitment that I would be "the first, but not the last" black person they hired.

I believed that I was invited to join, and joined the faculty to fill the school's need for a black teacher with sufficient experience, maturity, and commitment to persevere in the face of difficulties that, while undefined, would require all the ability and fortitude I could muster. I was to develop a substantive civil rights course, and I was to serve as a mentor and model for the black students. While I hoped to do research and writing, both the school and I recognized the enormous task I faced. No one expected that I would have time to publish prior to a tenure decision. A few faculty members felt I had scholarly potential, but emphasized that my pioneering role as teacher and representative of the black students should have priority.

A Reason for Protest

The Dimensions of the Challenge

Those early years were very demanding. I was determined to prove to the faculty that I was worthy of my position, utilizing the experience I had gained in practice along with my commitment to become a good teacher and a productive, if nontraditional scholar. But I seriously underestimated the degree to which faculty members conditioned real acceptance on academic credentials.

Initially, I had no interest in teaching courses in areas other than civil rights—and did so later (first Criminal Law and later Constitutional Law) only at the urging of the black students. In addition to broadening the areas in which I taught to assure them that I was "the real black law teacher" black students wanted, that is, one able to teach traditional courses as well as civil rights, I also spent countless hours listening to their problems, attending their meetings, even visiting those who took over buildings and classrooms. White students, noting that I was far more accessible than many of my white colleagues, eagerly joined the black students who wanted to discuss course work and school problems, or often just to spend some out-of-class time with a faculty member.

While my skill as a teacher improved, there was always the need—especially with first-year students—to overcome their apprehension that because I was the one black in an otherwise all-white faculty I might not be competent. It is a presumption that most minority teachers must face and overcome as they seek to teach students who, in all their lives, have never had black teachers. Resistance did not come only from white students. Some black students were afraid to take my courses for fear I would embarrass them by being less able than the white teachers. Others viewed me as a "double agent." Although I tried to be helpful, they made no distinction between me and the other members of the faculty, who were unfriendly and often patronizing to black students.

Fortunately, these doubters were in the minority. Most black students were proud of my presence and looked to me as a safe haven in an alien environment. I also found myself in the role of representative for a whole block of other minority and women students who had no faculty mentors at Harvard. For years, Latino students had been campaigning to persuade Harvard to hire a Latino faculty member. Three years after I arrived, the Law School hired a Latino lawyer, whose experience was impressive, as a part-time teaching fellow—the school's lowest rung—to lead a noncredit research and writing class. The teacher, Mario Obledo, left several months into the semester to become California's Secretary of Health, Education and Welfare.

It was not until that same year, 1972, that Harvard Law School hired its first woman for a full-time faculty position. Women students had pushed for someone with expertise in women's law issues. A few women were invited as visitors but were not offered permanent positions. At one faculty meeting a person for whom I have great respect responded to one woman's resume by saying: "When you tell me she graduated first in her class at Georgetown, I want to know whether she was the best person who finished at that school in the last five years. And, when you tell me she clerked for Court of Appeals Judge J. Skelly Wright, and then for Supreme Court Justice Thurgood Marshall, I come away unimpressed." Georgetown was not deemed a top-tier law school by those teaching at a school ranked at the top. Both Judge Wright and Justice Marshall, notwithstanding their considerable accomplishments on the bench, were regarded by the academic elite as bleeding-heart liberals and, thus, intellectually unimpressive. The candidate then, whatever her individual merits, was penalized for attending the wrong law school and accepting clerkships from the wrong judges.

Some faculty members who professed support for my role as a mentor and advocate for black students were less than delighted when I defined that role to include support for student protest programs, including representing at hearings those students facing disciplinary action for their participation in building takeovers and other activities considered beyond the pale. I remember several talks with Professor Charles Fried who, while troubled by my willingness to go to bat for students who had broken the school's rules, conceded reluctantly that it was perhaps what I had to do "for my constituency." To his credit, Fried, with whom I don't recall agreeing on any issue, did express his reservations to me personally. He was an above-board critic. You knew at all times that he was an opponent, which was much easier to deal with than the many who pledged to support diversity and then, in secret faculty votes, opposed every minority candidate.

Post-Confrontation Tenure

Despite the support of many faculty members, my own tenure was a close call. I had come to Harvard as a Lecturer-at-Law, with the understanding that the faculty would make a tenure decision in the latter part of my second year. After reviewing my record, the chair of the Appointments Committee, I think it was the late Professor Paul Bator, advised me that while my civil rights course was going well, they felt my course in Criminal Law—the course I had volunteered to teach to satisfy the black students—needed more work. They recommended that I postpone a tenure decision for another year. I didn't hesitate with my answer. Reminding them of the circumstances in which I had taught the Criminal Law course for two terms, I said that my appointment was for two years. I had worked hard during the period, and I now expected them to decide whether or not they would recommend me for tenure. When they made their decision, I would decide what I would do.

It proved the right response. A week or so later, Professor Bator told me that the Appointments Committee had decided to go to the faculty with a tenure recommendation. After a very long faculty meeting that, in accordance with tradition, I did not attend, Dean Sacks came to my office, also in accordance with long tradition, to report that the faculty had voted me a tenured position, subject only to the then pro-forma approval by Harvard's governing boards. Though pleased, I saw that the vote was a victory for me, but it did not necessarily advance my commitment to bringing true diversity to the faculty. If I did well, my success would lessen any obligation to look for other minorities. If I performed poorly, my failure would serve as an excuse to abandon further minority recruitment.

It was a dilemma with many dimensions. Faculty members expected that now that I was one of them, I would act like one of them. My ambivalence about this expectation of conformity manifested itself in humor with a double edge. For example, to celebrate my tenure, Dean Sacks and his wife, Delle, invited Jewel and me to their home for dinner. Several other faculty couples were also invited. After toasts were offered, I announced that, with tenure in hand, I was planning to purchase a car that I had always wanted: a white Cadillac convertible with red upholstery. In staid, understated Cambridge, my plan caused looks of pain and shock around the room. There was dead silence. Finally, much to everyone's relief, I told them that I was kidding. The joke, of course, was on me—an unconscious recognition of my profoundly discomforting role. Indeed, simply my presence on the faculty caused far more of a stir within the stately Harvard Law School community than had one of them begun driving the flamboyant car I told them I coveted.

I soon discovered that, whatever my willingness to conform, my tenured status did not entitle me to admission to the Law School's inner circles. My nontraditional teaching and writing seemed to confirm the faculty's doubts that a person without the usual credentials could be an able Harvard law professor. I found that the Socratic method, made famous by the book and movie *The Paper Chase*,[9] was inappropriate when the goal was not to terrify students into rote memorization and application of legal rules, but to teach them to think creatively and critically about the law. So, I experimented with teaching techniques that emphasized student participation and, to the dismay of some faculty members, even experimented with student self-grading. My publications were looked upon warily by faculty members who judged my area of civil rights peripheral to the main body of law, and my style of storytelling to be less rigorous than the doctrine-laden, citation-heavy law review pieces they favored.[10]

Despite glowing teaching reviews by my students, and a growing list of publications, including a civil rights text that became a standard in the field,[11] I had little success convincing the faculty that they should move promptly to appoint others like me. I should have expected this problem, which many other minority teachers have since confronted. With profoundly different experiences than the white, male professor, many of us bring to our jobs different styles and concerns. Students, though, while not reluctant to complain when a minority teacher departs from the style of white professors—a heresy they see as sufficiently suspect to warrant a trip to the dean's office—remain silent in the face of teaching they consider poor in white teachers' classes.

One example from my experience stands out. During my first year or so at Harvard, when I was still relatively unknown, Professor Adam Yarmolinsky, one of the Pentagon's "whiz kids" during the Kennedy administration, requested that I teach his Urban Issues class while he was attending a meeting in Washington. I agreed and, at the very start of the class, a student in the back raised his hand. "We are really disappointed in this course," he reported. "We expected new approaches on handling urban problems, but all we get is this mountain of readings and boring lectures." He spun out his complaints for several minutes. Then, a woman in the first row raised her hand. Hoping that she would point out to her classmate the inappropriateness of raising his complaint with me, I recognized her. I was wrong. "He's right," she said, motioning toward the student whose tirade she had interrupted. "This course has been a waste of time." I interrupted her: "I am certain Professor Yarmolinsky would be interested in your complaints." And, when I reported them to him, he was. The students had gone through several weeks of the course, disgruntled but unwilling to air their complaints until the white male professor was replaced for one class by his black counterpart.

What Yarmolinsky's students did was not necessarily racist, but it illustrates the double standard of evaluation that is no less devastating to minority teachers because it is unconsciously applied by some of their students. In Professor Yarmolinsky's class, I was simply a less intimidating figure to whom they felt free to voice their complaints. But when a black teacher seems less than ideal, students are similarly unintimidated when it comes to their end-of-term evaluations. As a result, a black teacher whose teaching is on a par with a white colleague's may receive less favorable marks simply because students do not challenge the white professor's presumption of competence. It is thus tough for minority teachers to be judged worthy of tenure by already suspicious professors, who give adverse student evaluations far more weight in our promotional evaluations than is the case for whites with traditional qualifications. Even when minority teachers gain tenure, any difference in our teaching or writing confounds our white colleagues, who still harbor doubts about our presence in their midst. Some redouble their resolve not to make the same mistake again.

"Where," Dean Bok asked when I reminded him of his promise that other blacks would follow me on the faculty, "are the Bill Hasties, Bill Colemans, and Charlie Houstons?" Each of these black men, Harvard Law alumni from earlier years, earned high grades and served on the prestigious *Harvard Law Review*,[12] but, I reminded Bok, the school had not hired any of them. What I didn't add is that I was outperforming many of those on the faculty with the credentials they so prized, some of whom had not published in years and, according to students' comments—usually far harsher than their official evaluations—left much to be desired as teachers. I did point out this fact to Dean Sacks several years later. He acknowledged that the work of some faculty members with outstanding resumes had been disappointing. He added quickly, though, that instances of disappointing performance are the reason Harvard had to adhere to traditional standards with even more rigor.

When in practice faculty members turn down candidates who have published well-regarded works because, on paper, they do not seem to have potential to write, they forfeit any claim of rationality. Their preferences make as much sense as passing up a respected welder to choose someone who has no experience but whose test scores show a mechanical aptitude. It is particularly frustrating and even more suspect because the credentials the faculty requires strongly correlate to upper-class standing.

Al Sacks himself was a good example of the phenomenon. He joined the faculty in 1952, after graduating from Harvard with high grades and a law review editorship. He served a clerkship on the Supreme Court. During his almost forty years on the faculty, Sacks gained great respect as a teacher and served with wisdom and dedication as dean during a very difficult period from 1971 to 1981. In any history of the Harvard Law School, there are few faculty members who made greater contributions to the school. Yet in the area of scholarly publications, the essential focus in faculty searches, Sacks did very little. His most important work, a set of readings on legal process written with Professor Henry Hart, was never published in a book.[13] The readings were distributed in mimeographed form for many years and used at a great number of schools, but Sacks lamented his failure to have them published when I went to his office and, in accordance with the school's custom, presented him with a copy of my book on civil rights law. I don't think anyone cared that he never published a book. There was a consensus: Al Sacks could do it if he wanted to. That was enough. The same acceptance was extended to several other faculty members whose scholarly promise far exceeded their performance.

While Harvard hires people who look good on paper even though their teaching and writing skills are untried, it regularly rejects black and other minority candidates with proven skills because their law school grades are not at the very top. I do not object to the faculty seeking and hiring blacks and other minorities whose high academic attainments seem to indicate the scholarly potential they prize, but it is both wrong and exclusionary to ignore those candidates who have achieved excellence in practice and in teaching—without having earned top grades at a few major law schools. A policy that elevates grades, a predictor of performance, over actual performance is illogical, unethical, exclusionary, and probably illegal.[14] This policy results in the exclusion of many potentially outstanding teachers, white as well as minority. Personally, the continual invoking of this policy was deeply disturbing. In finding these applicants unqualified, the school in effect was refusing to recognize, as I had always hoped, that my accomplishments as a teacher and writer justified giving serious consideration to other candidates with similar credentials.

I recall the responses of some faculty members to whom I have voiced this complaint. "Bell," they have told me, "your success is due to unusual talent and is hardly an argument against Harvard's traditional hiring standards." This assessment, deemed a compliment, is actually an insult. It bars me from using my hard-earned success as proof of what other blacks can do, and consigns me to a frustrating fate which most minority achievers recognize. When we excel, we are the exception, not the potential norm. Our success is, therefore, viewed as reason for faculty members to "thank our lucky stars," but not to hire other minority candidates. Woe, though, to the black professor who fails to produce what is regarded as an acceptable level of scholarship. He or she will be cited as good and sufficient reason for not hiring another minority teacher.

Combining Performance with Protest

Had I understood before accepting Harvard's offer how ingrained the hiring and tenure practices are, I likely would not have taken the job. Ignorance is sometimes a blessing. While those early years at Harvard

A Reason for Protest

exacted a physical and emotional cost, I enjoyed both teaching and writing. Harvard Law faculty enjoy access to resources, compensation, and prestige that is without parallel in legal education and seldom equaled in all of academe. I have found good students wherever I teach, but there is no denying the quality of Harvard's students. While I had gone into teaching to write, my relationships with students have been the most satisfying part of my teaching career. In fact, because so many students shared my desire for more diversity on the faculty, I began viewing them like the blacks I had represented across the South, people with few financial resources who risked jobs, homes, and even physical well-being in challenging segregation. Civil rights progress, they had taught me, required not only legal skills but also what they contributed: the willingness to take risks and make sacrifices. Harvard had not given me any reason to forget those lessons.

In the early seventies, several black law teachers came to the school for interviews and a few for visits. Despite my entreaties, none were offered full-time posts at Harvard. All ended up accepting positions elsewhere. After a few years of frustration, I wrote Dean Sacks in 1974 and sent copies of my letter to the Law School faculty. I announced that while I was powerless to make them honor their commitment to recruit and hire additional black faculty members, that year would be my last as the faculty's only black law teacher. In retrospect, this seems a bold and—given the lack of regard for my contribution there—a foolhardy step. But at the time, I felt it was essential either to share the burdens of black representation with someone else or leave before those burdens became overwhelming. My letter was not a threat but a declaration of the terms of my continuing to work at Harvard.

A few months later, the school hired its second black faculty member. Dean Sacks came by my office to report that an offer had been made and accepted by Clarence Clyde Ferguson, a 1951 Harvard graduate who had served on the Rutgers Law School faculty, been dean of the Howard Law School and Ambassador to Uganda. In reporting Ferguson's hiring, the Dean assured me that my letter had nothing to do with it. I didn't question his statement. As with so many civil rights advances, blacks are so happy to get them that we accept them without complaint or question. A third black man, Harry T. Edwards, now a federal court of appeals judge, joined the faculty a few years later. Even so, there was little change in either the pattern of appointments or the assumptions about academic qualifications that determined those appointments.

In 1979, I spent a sabbatical year as a visiting professor at the University of Washington Law School in Seattle. While there, Professor Eugene Scoles, whom I had met and gotten to know at law school conferences, invited me to visit his home law school at the University of Oregon. I did so, and through a series of events applied for and was named law school dean. Dean Sacks urged me not to go for all the right reasons: no time for teaching or scholarship, the need to raise funds and perform community public relations functions, and—worst of all—the obligation to try and keep faculty members content and as unobstructionist as possible.

But after eleven, tough years at Harvard, I was attracted by the warmth and congeniality of the much smaller school located in Eugene, a beautiful city. When offered the deanship there in 1980, I urged the faculty to consider the significance of hiring a black man committed to civil rights to head a mainly white law school in a state with no more than one or two percent black citizens. "We are ready," they assured me. "Are you?" I accepted the job. As it turned out, there was much that was positive about my deanship experience. Continuing budget troubles, though, made it difficult to implement my educational ideas and interfered, as well, with my plans to recruit and hire minority faculty.

The faculty did hire and later grant tenure to a black woman, Professor Linda Greene, but I soon learned that elitist hiring criteria are not unique to nationally recognized schools like Harvard. Oregon, too, was apprehensive about hiring applicants with impressive experience in practice or teaching at other schools unless they also had earned high grades at a prestigious law school. Never mind that many of them had more modest credentials. More than any specific appointment, it was this propensity for equating the best qualified candidates with elite academic credentials that would lead to my resignation.

For me, the final straw came when the faculty voted not to authorize me to offer a position to Pat Chew, an Asian-American woman who had graduated high in her class at the University of Texas Law School. Chew, now a full professor at the University of Pittsburgh Law School, spoke Chinese and had gained experience through law practice with the many legal problems in doing business with Pacific Rim countries. Both the school and the community would have benefitted from her expertise. In addition, Asians are the Oregon Law School's largest minority group. We had reviewed more than one hundred candidates and listed Chew as our third choice behind two white males with fancier credentials but, as I recall, no practice experience. Both rejected our offers. In an hours-long faculty meeting, a few professors convinced a majority that "we could do better" and urged that we reopen the search. All were aware of my strong support for Chew. I promised to honor the vote and not extend Chew an offer, but told them that I was stepping down so that they could select as dean someone whose leadership they were ready to follow.

There was more frustration than wisdom in this statement. Law school faculties are seldom ready to follow anyone's leadership. Had I fought for Chew, perhaps seeking assistance at the university level, I could have gained authority to extend her an offer. Oregon's faculty, while not easy to lead, were probably better than many. They were seriously underpaid, taught more hours than most law teachers, and because of their attachment to the state's beautiful vistas and temperate climate, were exploited by state officials who assumed—incorrectly in many instances—that no other school would take them, even if they decided to leave Oregon.

My attitude did not help our relationship. When I encountered the predictable resistance to some of my suggestions, I rather too quickly responded with the reminder that I had taken the deanship as a favor to them and the school. And, at any time that they decided that my presence was no longer a benefit, they should let me know and I would return to Harvard. In retrospect, my statement expressed my frustration, rather than any good judgment or political sense.

At the time of my departure from Harvard, there was one black man and one white woman among its sixty-person tenured faculty—which student protesters decried often as "one sorry situation." The students intensified their struggle for more black faculty. In part to respond to these demands, Dean Vorenberg, who had succeeded Albert Sacks as law school dean, asked whether I might come back to teach my civil rights course during the winter term—a special, one-month semester held in January. I reminded him that I was now a dean myself and owed my allegiance to Oregon. There were, moreover, any number of black lawyers fully capable of teaching my course. Subsequently, Vorenberg hired Jack Greenberg, then the NAACP Legal Defense Fund's Director Counsel, and Julius Chambers, chair of the organization's board of directors, to teach a civil rights course during the 1983 spring term. Both were outstanding lawyers, but the black students were quite upset. They felt the position should serve as a trial period for a black teacher who might then be offered a full-time position. Neither Greenberg nor Chambers were potential candidates for permanent positions. A black law student leader, Muhammed Kenyatta, wrote Greenberg urging him not to accept the position. Among several reasons, he suggested that, as a white man, Greenberg could not serve as a role model for black students. This charge was picked up by the media, which had a field day accusing the black students of "reverse racism" and ingratitude given Greenberg's long record of working for black equality.[15]

To their credit, the black students were not intimidated. They boycotted the Greenberg-Chambers offering and developed their own course on racism and the law. With financial support from Dean Vorenberg, they arranged for a number of minority scholars and practitioners to lecture. In the wake of the boycott, on December 15, 1982, the faculty adopted a resolution declaring that legal education is "served best" by a faculty with a "variety of perspectives" and that minorities and women "historically have been and still continue to be too few" at Harvard and other law schools. The resolution committed the faculty to making special efforts to recruit minority and women professors. The faculty also approved a report from the Appointments Committee recommending affirmative action to "seek out faculty prospects among minorities and women" until the faculty votes that "there no longer exists a significant problem."[16]

Through sit-ins and other protests, students continued to pressure Harvard to hire full-time black professors. Two young black men, Christopher Edley, Jr., in 1981, and Randall Kennedy in 1984, joined the faculty, and a third, David Wilkins, accepted an offer in 1986. All three men held credentials—membership on Harvard's or Yale's law review, and Supreme Court clerkships—that made them acceptable to their white colleagues. Even so, student pressure played an important role in each of these appointments, as it presumably did in helping Dean James Vorenberg persuade the faculty to offer me a new position even before I resigned my deanship at Oregon in 1985. In deciding to return, I hoped this offer reflected the long-awaited reforms for which so many students had pushed for so long. It did not take long to realize that attitudes regarding minority hiring had not changed. In addition, the faculty was now locked in an ideological struggle that pushed issues of minority hiring almost off the faculty agenda.

THREE

A Campaign That Failed

*Xercis, as Protector, ruled the Citadel's extended domain. By tra-
dition, he sought guidance and concurrence from the Council of Elders. The elders were a small, select group who, along with the Protector's family, constituted the Citadel's leaders. Admission to the
Council was limited to the most gifted children of Council members
and other leaders, all of whom were outstanding graduates of an elite
preparatory school. A certain number of these graduates were chosen
to become apprentices to Council Elders, and some of this group were
later sponsored by an Elder for beginning leadership roles. This procedure led to the selection of Elders, some able and others not. All were,
not remarkably, almost identical in background, education, and opinion. All were male. No woman had ever been considered for these roles.
Indeed, most of the Elders were finding it hard to imagine a woman
on the Council, much less as Protector, even one as accomplished as
Tamar, their own Protector's daughter.*

*Even more far-fetched was the notion that a lowlander could be
present in the Council's sessions, let alone speak or cast a vote as a
Council member. Yet exactly that was what the lowlanders were now
demanding. Having never sat in the ruling Council, the lowlanders
assumed that their voices and votes would ensure that their interests
would be represented and accommodated. And to achieve that aim,
they were engaging in an array of nonviolent protests, sitdown strikes,
disruptive marches, and roadside blockades.*

CONFRONTING AUTHORITY

Upon first hearing the lowlanders' demand for representation, Xercis and the Council of Elders rejected it out of hand. Lowlanders, possessing none of the traditional traits that were prerequisites for admission, were not fitted to make serious decisions affecting the well-being of untold thousands. This answer Xercis communicated to the lowlanders' leaders; he expected that they would accept it, see reason, and subside. But Xercis' answer only infuriated the lowlanders and led thousands more to join the ranks of the protesters. Within a week, they gathered at the bottom of the Citadel mountain, surrounded it, and refused to allow any one to pass through their unarmed but determined ranks.

Xercis and the Council met to consider how to send the lowlanders back to work and to restore order. The Citadel had superior arms, and some Elders urged that the revolt be put down by force. But other Elders suspected—as many a repressive regime has found out to its cost—that resorting to force to quell a peaceful protest might only heighten the rebels' fervor. These Elders counselled patience, predicting that the rebels would tire of their blockade and return to the relative comfort of their homes. All looked to Xercis for his decision.

If there was one event that gave advocates of faculty diversity reason for optimism in the otherwise turbulent years following the 1987 conservative revolt at Harvard, which denied tenure to two left-leaning scholars, it was the invitation to Professor Regina Austin to be a visiting scholar for the 1989–90 school year. I was enthusiastic about Austin and what I thought her visit would portend for Harvard Law School. She was, as I told a student group when I introduced her for a lecture several months before her visit, ideally prepared to carry out the responsibilities of the black law teacher today. She could do all that our white colleagues do—teach with both skill and sensitivity for all our students. And in our writing, she could teach us to express perspectives based on our experience that enable us to better understand our condition, explain our status to the world, and contribute as we can to the on-going, never-ending effort to gain for all people of color that recognition for our citizenship, our contributions, our humanity which so many in this society seem so determined to deny.

On the day Austin arrived, I suggested we attend the faculty lunch where a professor would be discussing a work in progress. As it turned out, the presenter was Charles Fried, recently returned to Harvard after serving from 1985 to 1989 as solicitor general in the Reagan administration. Early in his talk on—of all things—affirmative action, Fried observed sagely that as a result of recent Supreme Court decisions raising standards of proof in race discrimination cases, we were now witnessing the interesting paradox that women charging gender discrimination would have an easier time proving their cases than would blacks. He began elaborating on what he obviously saw as a significant development when Austin interrupted him: "You are really only talking about white women, aren't you?" Fried was taken aback. "What, what?" he stammered. "I said," Austin repeated firmly, "that when you talk about women having an easier time proving their cases under current law, you are talking about white women." Her point, of course, was that black women's claims would be measured by the stiffer standards of proof required for race discrimination cases, even when their claims were based on sex as well as race.

There was a moment of embarrassed silence. It was obvious that Fried had simply not considered black women in speaking of "women" as a category in race discrimination law. He was not alone. It was the first, but far from the last, time during her visit that Austin introduced a much-needed perspective both in her classes and in informal talks with faculty. Neither Fried nor most of the faculty members at that first luncheon had yet met Austin personally. They met her now in a challenging role that was to become her hallmark. Finally, Fried pulled himself together. "I see your point," he acknowledged with a pained smile. He continued with his presentation, for once stripped of the air of intellectual invincibility that both his voice and manner seemed to convey. I thought it was a triumphal moment for Austin and an indication of what her presence would mean to us all. Evidently, a substantial majority of the faculty were less ready than I was for a black woman who had a keen insight about sex and race roles in the society and was more than willing to challenge traditional male views regarding these issues.

Austin, a 1973 honors graduate from the University of Pennsylvania Law School, served as an associate with a large Philadelphia law firm for three years and then joined the University of Pennsylvania law faculty in 1977, gaining promotion to a tenured position in 1983. Those credentials—particularly her years as a successful teacher—convinced me that Austin was a veteran able to survive in her very difficult pioneering role at Harvard. In appreciation of her teaching, Austin's first-year Torts students at Penn had filled her office with a toy train and other symbols of the railway cases and legal principles they had learned in her classes. Her Torts class at Harvard also went well, though she tended to recognize minority and women students first rather than last or not at all, as happened in some first-year classes. Some white male students resented this departure from the classroom norm and complained of the favoritism they ignored in other classes when they were its beneficiaries. Their resentment was expressed in negative student evaluations at the end of the year.

During the year, though, I thought Austin's visit was proceeding well. She was a hit with the minority students, particularly the women, and gained the grudging respect of many of the white women as well, despite—or perhaps because of—her willingness to speak her mind on sensitive issues of race and feminism. Austin had published only a few pieces in her early years of teaching, a fact that her detractors regarded as the academic equivalent of cardinal sin. They ignored her more recent writing, which some of us found exciting. Austin exhibited keen insight in her interpretations of contemporary racial and gender barriers that, while apparently fair and objective, actually maintained old discriminatory patterns with a silent

A Campaign That Failed

and even more invidious effect. I was concerned that many on the faculty might miss this aspect of her writing, and in February 1990 I praised her work in a memo to the Appointments Committee, urging that they recommend her for a permanent appointment.

I focused on her most recent article, "Sapphire Bound!," in which she considered the case of a young, unmarried black woman who was fired from her job as a youth counselor when she became pregnant.[1] Her dismissal was justified by her employer's "negative role model rule," requiring the immediate discharge of staff members who set a bad example for their charges.[2]

In "Sapphire Bound!," Austin urged scholars to take on the enormous "task of capturing the complexity of [minority women's] legal status and of translating their concerns into those that the legal scholarly community recognizes"—a task that otherwise had been shamefully neglected. Austin's analysis of the particular dilemma the *Chambers* case raised was from a perspective that no white professor had taken. I must admit that a year or so before, when I covered the case in my class, I would have found it difficult to defend an employee who intentionally became pregnant in violation of her employer's specific and seemingly understandable rule against unwed pregnancies.

Austin made a different point:

> For those who have no understanding of the historical oppression of black women and no appreciation of the diversity of their contemporary cultural practices, the outcome of the *Chambers* case might have a certain policy appeal, one born of sympathy for poor black youngsters and desperation about stemming "the epidemic" of teenage pregnancy that plagues them. According to such an assessment, the Club's hope that its members could be influenced by committed counselors who, by example, would prove that life offers more attractive alternatives than early pregnancy and single parenthood is at worst benign, if it is not benevolent.

But for better informed, more critical evaluators, the opinions are profoundly disturbing. Firing a young unmarried, pregnant black worker in the name of protecting other young black females from the limited options associated with early and unwed motherhood is ironic, to say the least. The Club managed to replicate the very economic hardships and social biases that, according to the district court, made the role model rule necessary in the first place. Crystal Chambers was not much older than some of the Club members and her financial and social status after being fired was probably not that much different from what the members would face if they became pregnant at an early age, without the benefit of a job or the assistance of a fully employed helpmate. On the other hand, she was in many respects better off than many teen mothers. She was in her early twenties, had a decent job, and planned her pregnancy. Chambers' condition became problematic because of the enforcement of the role model rule.[3]

I advised the Appointments Committee that Austin's analysis had a profound effect on many of my students. While not every student embraced her views or appreciated her outspokenness on race and gender, those positions needed to be heard, and I urged them to do whatever was necessary to retain Austin.

My memo, which stated the major arguments of the students and faculty who wanted Austin on our permanent faculty, became a symbol of my inability to convince the faculty to act on racial matters of the most basic concern to me. Not one member of the Appointments Committee responded substantively to my memo. When I raised the issue during a faculty meeting, Robert Clark, who had been named dean in 1989, responded that because of the faculty policy deferring tenure votes on visitors during the year of their residence, we would have to delay consideration of Austin until the following year.

A Campaign That Failed

The visitor deferral policy—one observed only periodically in the past, and not observed when Clark was given a permanent faculty position during his 1977–78 visit from the Yale Law School—became the administration's main response to student pleas that the faculty act immediately on Austin's appointment. Whatever the reasons had been for adopting this policy, students and I argued that it was both unfair and unwise to apply it to visitors who were members of groups that were not represented, or seriously underrepresented, on the faculty.

It is unfair because, at the very least, the policy allows lengthy delays in compensating for the current nonrepresentation of black women, Latinos, Asians, Native Americans, gays and lesbians, and the physically disabled, to cite the groups represented in the Coalition for Civil Rights, a student organization which spearheaded the diversity movement. It is unwise because visitors who are members of unrepresented groups, and whose credentials and performance were sufficient to gain them a visit at Harvard, will also be seriously sought after by other schools. Indeed, their presence as Harvard visitors will likely help generate permanent offers from other schools. This had been the case with other minority visitors, and, since arriving at Harvard, Austin had received a tenure offer from Michigan and a visiting offer from Stanford. Since the school claimed that the policy was enacted to spare visitors the discomfort of being evaluated while still on campus, we at least asked that minority candidates be allowed to elect to be considered immediately.

The "we might lose her to another school" argument didn't move anyone, nor did my "what if I were hit by a truck" scenario. I had embellished it over the years so that, by 1990, it sounded something like this: "If by some combination of unexpected calamities none of the five black men now on the faculty were able to teach for the next several years, all would deem our loss a crisis. The faculty would quickly reach a consensus that minority replacements—women as well as men—must be found and pressed into service. Yet that is precisely the position we are in with no tenured black women or other unrepresented minorities on the premises. Martin Luther King used the analogy of a red traffic light: while they are generally a good idea, you don't expect ambulances on their way to an emergency to stop for them.

That argument usually made faculty members' eyes glaze over or provoked comments about my macabre sense of humor. With mock seriousness, friends urged me to be careful crossing busy streets. They need not have worried. Even when I was the sole black on the faculty, I was not willing to get myself killed in order to prove that they would promptly seek another minority candidate—preferably someone who met their cherished criteria, although a noncredentialed scholar, if necessary—to replace me. Now that there were five black men on the faculty, the faculty saw no need to respond to the usual pleas for greater diversity. The notion that the absence of women among those faces should be a matter of serious concern was simply beyond their comprehension.

Black women were simply ignored or forgotten. Like Charles Fried, most faculty members thought of two separate groups seeking protection: blacks and women. Harvard Law School could consider itself covered because each group was represented on its faculty. A slogan displayed on tee-shirts worn by black women students during one of their diversity protests reflected their plight: "All the women are white, all the blacks are men, but some of us are brave."[4] The fact that so few considered it a problem was itself a powerful argument for the need to hire a woman of color. Disregarded by an indifferent faculty was my best and most deeply felt argument for hiring minority women for our faculty. As I wrote Dean Clark in giving notice of my intention to take a protest leave of absence:

Although I have never forgotten my representational function on this faculty, I was slow to recognize that as a black man, I am not able to understand, interpret, and articulate the very unique conditions and challenges black women face. While I urged the hiring of black women, I thought that as a black man I could both comprehend and represent the needs and interests of black women. A modicum of exposure to feminist writings, particularly those by black women, and Regina Austin's presence and effectiveness have disabused me of this unintended but no less inexcusable presumptuousness. The large role our black women students are playing in the recent diversity protests here confirm their recognition of what should have been obvious to me years ago.

I wish the push for women of color on the faculty was simply a matter of seeking conformity with a currently popular social goal. It is not. As each day's newspapers reveal and a flood of studies confirm, black and Hispanic men are faring quite poorly in contemporary society. It is not fortuitous that—despite the best efforts of our admissions office—there are many more women than men of color in our student body. The disparity is larger at the college level and is most obvious at black colleges, where the ratio of black women to black men is often five and six to one. We simply must do justice by our black and Hispanic women, for it appears they will have to handle an ever-increasing share of the leadership role in the 1990s and beyond.[5]

Students were busy pressing the same concerns. They had petitioned the faculty, met with them individually, and plied them with names of minority women who were doing significant work at other law schools. Gaining little more from their efforts than vague promises to continue seeking qualified candidates, the students organized themselves into the Coalition for Civil Rights, and turned to rallies, silent vigils outside faculty meetings, and overnight sit-ins in the dean's office.

These tactics had been effective in the past, when satisfying our claims was regarded as either morally right or politically prudent. Times had changed since I joined the faculty, and students now found themselves facing a much less sympathetic audience. Students made little headway with a quite conservative dean and a cadre of faculty members organized to save the school from excessively liberal faculty members and the further erosion of what they viewed as traditional hiring standards. Affirmative action, once generally regarded as a legitimate, if only partial, repayment of society's debt to black people, was now looked upon as an unfounded claim, one put forward by those who otherwise did not deserve the jobs they sought.[6] Alan Dershowitz stated this position vigorously at every opportunity, and a substantial number of faculty members agreed with this view—if not often with Dershowitz's articulation of it. It was no surprise, then, that the students' protests resulted in warnings of disciplinary action rather than in the Law School's commitment to hiring minorities.

As is often the case when an institution's policies are challenged, the administration focused on issues of security and rule compliance, rather than on the students' goals. While I feared that dean's office takeovers and similarly disruptive actions were not productive and merely shifted attention from the real issues, I always visited and supported students taking part in these exercises, bringing them blankets at night and breakfast in the mornings.

In the early Spring of 1990, I learned that the coalition of students leading the diversity effort were considering a plan to take their final exams in the Spring, but then to place them in escrow, rather than turn them in for grading, pending a substantive commitment by the Law School to hire more minorities. Here, I thought, was a protest the school could not ignore. Without all final exams in hand, professors would have a difficult time grading, always a herculean task under the best of circumstances. Without all final grades, the school could not compute class standings and allocate awards. Indeed, it would not even know which third-year students joining the plan had enough credits to graduate. Of course, the school could give failing grades and refuse degrees to all students who refused to turn in their final exams. Given the students' reason for withholding their exams, though, such an act would almost certainly bring down criticism from parents and alumni, including those not particularly interested in faculty diversity.

The Coalition, it seemed to me, had grasped the secret of effective civil rights protest: for strong moral reasons, protesters withhold their participation in order to stop business as usual among those whose policies they seek to change. As far back as the 1930s, blacks living in large, urban areas had used such tactics to good effect. The Buying Power Movement, which began in Chicago before the Depression and soon spread to other cities, successfully employed boycotts, pickets, and demonstrations to convince white-run businesses with large black markets that it would be in their best economic interest to hire black employees.[7] In New York, boycott protests led by the Reverend Adam Clayton Powell, Jr., later a Congressman for the area, added ten thousand jobs for blacks in just four years.[8] In 1941, the prominent labor leader A. Philip Randolph threatened a march on Washington by Negro and liberal forces, causing President Roosevelt to issue an executive order outlawing discrimination in defense industries.[9] Again, in the 1950s and 1960s, the boycott was used over and over by civil rights demonstrators seeking to end Jim Crow practices and force merchants to hire and serve blacks on the same basis as whites.[10] The organized efforts of the black citizens of Montgomery, Alabama, who for a year stayed off of the city's segregated buses, finally broke the resistance of white officials and contributed to the integration of public facilities across the country.[11]

More recently, this tactic has been resurrected with some success by the Reverend Jesse Jackson's Operation PUSH.[12] It has been behind a number of recent boycotts of major corporations—including Nike, the sneaker manufacturer which draws much of its $2 billion income from black customers, but had no black board members and does business with few black companies. Although Nike denied that its actions were in response to the boycott, it quickly named a black coach to its board and appointed a black vice president.[13] Before the Nike action, Operation PUSH employed similar campaigns to force major companies, like Coca-Cola and Anheuser-Busch, to agree to spend hundreds of millions of dollars in the black community through jobs and purchases from black vendors. Organized labor has also used the boycott, with generally good results. In the 1960s and 1970s, a campaign was waged to stop consumers from buying grapes in order to force growers to improve migrant workers' wages and working conditions, and in the 1980s the Adolph Coors Company was nearly ruined when the AFL-CIO called a boycott to support the company's striking workers. Coors lost $20 million in profits over seven years, and eventually agreed not to oppose unionization of its work force.[14] When the NAACP threatened a boycott by civil rights organizations, Coors negotiated a plan to hire and promote blacks and to do business with black companies, which would create $325 million in income for blacks.[15]

For reasons I found difficult to comprehend, students ready to risk going to jail by invading the dean's office were less ready to pledge their participation in the escrow plan. As I understand it, a letter announcing the exam-escrow plan was drafted and circulated for signatures. It was agreed that the letter would not be made public unless at least one hundred students signed it.

Unknown to the students, by that point I had already written Dean Clark a letter and sent copies to the faculty announcing my intention to take a leave until the faculty hired and tenured a woman of color. As I had with the similar letter I wrote in 1974, announcing that it would be my last year as the only black faculty member, I distributed it on a confidential basis, hoping to prompt a private faculty discussion and resolution of the matter. In keeping with what I had come to see as Harvard's standard policy in respect to my letters, I received no response from Dean Clark or anyone on the Appointments Committee. A few faculty colleagues expressed their support, though I remember best those whose comments were phrased as what I called "count me out" questions, like "How are you going to pay your bills?" Instead of inspiring the supportive action of other faculty members, my assertion that I would go on unpaid leave in support of my belief in diversity seemed to distance me from friends and foes alike—hardly what I either expected or needed.

I can't recall another period during my long career at Harvard when I felt more frustrated by the school's failure even to take my position seriously. They knew they had the power to simply ignore me while keeping most of the students content with promises and platitudes. While I could not overturn the faculty's authority, my willingness to risk my position gave me the power to turn their refusal into an embarrassment. After two weeks without a formal reply from the dean, and with no stirring of faculty support, I recognized that the school would have to feel more pressure than I could generate. I told the Coalition leaders of my planned protest leave and authorized them to announce my plans publicly in whatever way they felt would help the diversity campaign. I hoped that, among other things, my planned leave might encourage students to sign the exams-in-escrow letter. When asked by students what they should do, I never failed to remind them of the already planned boycott. Student support for my protest was overwhelming, but the number of students signing the escrow letter never exceeded thirty-seven. Actually, this was a sufficient number for an effective protest, but it was not enough to provide the signers with what student leader Keith Boykin described as a "critical mass minimum" needed to protect them. The exam-escrow plan died.

Many readers may conclude that the exam-escrow plan was wrong, deserved to fail, and that my encouragement violated my duties as a member of the faculty. Such charges simply highlight the dilemma faced by many blacks who are committed to eliminating discrimination and who occupy positions in organizations whose policies serve to disadvantage minorities. Where does our primary allegiance lie? In my case, the Law School granted me a lifetime position at a good salary and generous benefits, yet I had accepted the position on the clear understanding that I could also pioneer racial diversification of the faculty. I knew from long experience that virtually all racial advances in this country have taken place as a response to disruptive activity—or its likelihood—that posed a threat to the status quo. This had been the case with the lunch counter sit-ins and the later voting rights marches, and, in the past, at the Harvard Law School itself. I resolved my conflicting allegiances by giving priority to my commitment to faculty diversity and doing so in a manner that, if I failed, my faculty position would be terminated.

In retrospect, I see an uncomfortable parallel between the willingness of students to take over the dean's office but not place their grades in jeopardy, and my willingness to take an unpaid leave but not launch an even more risky protest. The students did not expect their occupancy of the dean's office to result in more than a disciplinary hearing and, perhaps, a letter of reprimand in their permanent files. It was unlikely the local police would be called or that the school would actually prosecute students for a peaceful office takeover. On the other hand, their refusal to turn in final exam papers placed in jeopardy credit for courses in which they had worked hard, and they were unwilling to risk a failing grade, or even possible expulsion, which would require the immediate repayment of their student loans. John Bonifaz, one of the student leaders who signed the letter, later paraphrased the view of many students: "There was a wrong that needed to be righted, but not at the expense of being thrown out of Harvard."

Similarly, while my protest leave was a dramatic gesture, I felt fairly sure that with substantial effort, I could maintain myself and my obligations. If, on the other hand, I had taken literally what I referred to in announcing my protest to a student rally as a "financial fast," I could have refused income from any source. Or, by going on a hunger strike, I could have placed my health as well as my finances in jeopardy. I did neither. Neither action was likely to equal the social pressures generated in the late 1960s after Martin Luther King's assassination. Protests that exceed in risk and danger the aims they hope to accomplish tend to overshadow protest goals. Protesters—already suspect for breaching the norms of civil conduct—are easily labeled and dismissed as fanatics.

While face-saving rationales are comforting, it is also likely that neither the students' exam-escrow plan nor a life-threatening hunger strike would have moved the faculty to the action we sought. The presence of five black men on the faculty, each performing very well, served as an insulation against charges that the Law School was discriminating against minorities. The school could also point to the few black women and Latino teachers who were invited for one-year visits. Although none of them had gained permanent positions, they seemingly were always under consideration—complacency-inviting proof of good faith and the never-met promise of change. In a speech at a student rally, Professor Duncan Kennedy derisively called this system "rotating diversity."

When I announced my protest leave at a rally organized by students, front page articles in the *New York Times* and the *Boston Globe* triggered nationwide press coverage.[16] None of my previous protests had garnered so much attention. For the next several days, I talked with television and print media reporters around the clock; I always insisted that the student leaders be involved in television interviews. The Reverend Jesse Jackson accepted the students' invitation to speak and to help negotiate my differences with the Law School. While Dean Clark reluctantly met with Jackson prior to a press conference-rally, he firmly refused to negotiate through him. Jackson's presence made for a full house of students and media people in Austin Hall where the press conference was scheduled. For about ten minutes before the conference, Jackson sat in my office taking notes on a yellow pad as student leaders and I briefed him on the protest activities and goals. At the conference, Jackson conveyed complete familiarity with the protest, and his presentation was a marvel of advocacy. "To say," Jackson thundered, "that in 1990 there is no black woman anywhere in America qualified to be a tenured faculty member is both an error and a gross insult to our intelligence."[17]

But neither Jackson at his rhetorical best, nor the continued efforts of students and some alumni, budged the law school from its long-held position. Dean Clark maintained that the school must follow its traditional hiring procedures, but a letter signed by 502 Harvard Law students and published in the *Boston Globe*, responded: "We ask how a procedure which for 350 years has perpetuated uniformity will now produce diversity."[18] Tenured faculty members argued, as they had since almost the first days of the protest, that they could not find a single woman of color whose appointment to the faculty would not irredeemably compromise Harvard's high standards of excellence.

Although the criteria of outstanding grades and prestigious judicial clerkships may identify potential erudite teachers with the ability to expound upon jurisprudence in time-honored fashion, it is a poor measure of the willingness and ability to prepare students to function in a more diverse and complicated society. Meeting the needs of students who come from an increasingly wide variety of life experiences requires skills that are not identified by the existing hiring formula. Especially today, when the greedy self-interest of many practicing attorneys has plunged the profession to new depths of ill-repute, training lawyers to assume a role of supposedly public trust calls upon us to emphasize skills and experiences the Law School ignores in its hiring process.

Professor Regina Austin described the need when she wrote:

[W]omen of color in this society are bearing a terrible burden. Black women are laboring away in the back offices of large financial institutions because their lovely brown faces are thought to be bad for business. We know little about the working lives and legal problems of the Asian women who populate stitch shops and massage parlors. Young Latino women are dropping out of school at an alarming rate with hardly a peep from the rest of us. Native American women are attacked for their alcoholism in ways that recall stereotypes long associated with [what] colonizing white men dubbed "Indians." Behind the students' actions there is hope born of a generous impulse that they could do more for such women if only they were better taught about what needs to be done.[19]

University Professor Frank Michelman, possessing an empathy so sadly lacking both on issues of diversity and the other racial problems that daily become more serious and more threatening at Harvard and around the nation, prepared an eloquent statement for a student rally. He said:

> My views about faculty diversity are pretty simple. It's a matter of excellence combined with simple justice. Simple justice means not forgetting matters of history, national and local, that we haven't yet earned the right to forget. Excellence means making Harvard Law School the best it can be.
>
> I doubt that our faculty as it now is, with its small numbers of people who are not white and who are not men, does or can excellently satisfy the real educational needs and requirements of all of our students. Education here would be more excellent if our faculty's composition better responded to our student body's full range of backgrounds and experiences, perceptions and sensibilities, interests and concerns, plans and purposes. On the scholarship front, excellence means—among other things— inclusion of the full variety of legal scholarly talents, visions, and projects that merit recognition and a chance to be further developed, displayed, and shared here.[20]

Eloquence in the cause of diversity is inspiring but inadequate to overturn deeply fixed hiring and tenure policies. Regina Austin, notwithstanding all our efforts—and for a time, she and others felt, *because* of our efforts—was not offered a tenured position at the Harvard Law School. By any definition, this was a failure, one that may have injured the individual the students and I were trying to help, while leaving unchanged, even unmoved, the institution we wanted to reform.

FOUR

Year One: Protest in Residence

Tamar, though not eligible to attend the critical meeting of the Council of Elders, made it clear to her father whose side she was on.

"But you do not understand," Xercis had protested to his daughter. "It is not merely that the lowlanders are a different people. Our method of choosing leaders provides the Citadel with stability based on the recognition of ability and the reward of achievement." Xercis could not keep the irritation out of his voice.

Tamar looked across the great table in his chambers and smiled at him. "And the apprentices, those from whom the elders are chosen, how are they selected?" she asked. It was a question to which they both knew the answer. "Suppose, father, that we allowed those who were unrelated or unconnected to the elders to serve in these positions? Suppose, even, that we searched across the land for our apprentices?"

"Daughter,"—again exasperation sharpened his voice—"I am no love-besmitten prince chasing across the land looking for a Cinderella whose foot will fit a glass slipper. What you suggest would simply raise hopes that would be cruelly dashed. You know as well as I about the gap in schooling, the great differences in culture."

"All true," Tamar acknowledged, "but merit, father, is out there. New blood. Intelligent, if less well-schooled. Courageous, if not as attuned to our patrician tastes. There are men and women out there

67

who could breathe new life into our dusty halls. And," she added in warning, "give new hope to the lowlanders. Their rage is growing. They will not abandon their blockade, and those who would break their peaceful protest with violence will play into the rebels' hands."

Xercis sighed. How had he, the very soul of moderation, come to have such a daughter, one who seemed bent on challenging his authority?

By the time I decided on the form of my protest, it was too late to obtain a visiting position elsewhere, but I had decided even before the 1989–90 school year ended to remain at Harvard rather than seek a visiting offer at another law school. Jewel's battle with cancer required us to remain close to her doctors in Boston. Even were a visit feasible, I feared that my absence would dilute the effectiveness of my protest. I could almost hear faculty critics carping, "If he wanted to go away for a visit, why didn't he just do it and not cause such a fuss?"

Summer-long efforts to forestall my protest leave through negotiations brokered by Professor Roger Fisher had not succeeded. Fisher, the co-author of the bestseller *Getting to Yes*,[1] had mediated contentious conflicts in the Middle East and around the world, but he and his staff were unable to work out a mutually acceptable settlement in my case. While I tried to remain flexible, I insisted that Harvard commit to a few steps that would have some real possibility of diversifying the faculty. When the dean and faculty proved unwilling to do more than make a few vague promises, I settled in for at least a full year of protest.

In response to the statements of students who praised my protest but expressed regret that they would not be able to enroll in my courses, I offered to teach my civil rights seminar without pay to those willing to take the course without receiving grades or credit. Reluctantly, and with more than a little suspicion, Dean Clark agreed to this arrangement. As it turned out, teaching a group of twenty-five or so students, each of whom was doing a substantial amount of preparation every week for a course that would not count towards their degree, was very fulfilling for me, and, I think, for them as well. Each of us had the satisfaction of knowing that we were there, not for credit or pay, but because we all *wanted* to be there. It was an unexpected but rewarding dividend of my protest.

I had often said that I enjoyed teaching law enough to do it for free. The protest gave me an opportunity to put my money where my mouth was. It was a marvelous experience, but it was not easy. In addition to teaching the course, I met with students, reviewed their papers, and even attended faculty meetings. I also had taken on a heavy load of outside lectures to substitute for the Harvard salary I would not receive. Fortunately, the lecture invitations continued to arrive. My appreciation was heightened by the knowledge that this warm response, particularly from the law school and university communities, might have been quite different.

Given the number of friends and supporters who pull away from the solo protester, those who remain steadfast and supportive are especially valued. Some rise to the occasion and join your struggle despite their better judgment or their disagreement with your tactics. After I had announced my Harvard protest, Assistant Professor Charles Ogletree—at the time, the only untenured black faculty member—called me that evening to tell me that after discussing the matter with his wife, Pam, he wanted me to know that if I wanted him to join my protest leave, he was ready to do so. This was a most welcome offer and I was tempted to welcome him aboard. Then, considering his untenured status, I thanked him, pointing out that the school expected him to launch a clinical program in criminal law in the Fall. He accepted my assessment, but Ogletree has been a mainstay of support throughout the years of my protest. In addition, he has assumed much of my role of working with minority students at the Law School.

Across the country, a long-time friend, Professor Charles Lawrence, organized a student-faculty protest at the Stanford Law School in support of my stand.[2] The following year, Lawrence took a leave from Stanford to protest its minority hiring practices, including its failure to offer permanent positions to any of the minority women the school willingly invited for visits. Lawrence subsequently resigned and is now a tenured member of the Georgetown Law School faculty, a school that has managed to find, hire, and tenure no less than six minority women professors.[3]

About a week after I announced my protest, Jewel and I had our spirits lifted tremendously by a telephone call from a major entertainment figure—one who from the start insisted on anonymity. He reported that he supported my stand wholeheartedly and that while I was on unpaid leave he was willing to put me on his "shadow legal staff" to ensure that I would not miss a "financial beat" during my leave. I called back later to again express my appreciation, but to say that I didn't think I would need financial assistance. The following week, the entertainer's staff person called and offered me a consultant's position with his writers. I accepted on condition that it was a serious offer of work. I was assured it was. During my consultancy, I sent down a stream of memos filled with suggestions that, in retrospect, were not appropriate for his work, but a few ideas did appear and reassured me that someone was at least reading my contributions. The money I was paid did not replace my salary, but it certainly gave a boost to my budget and my morale.

The Reverend Dr. Peter Gomes, Harvard's Plummer Professor of Christian Morals and Minister to the University Church, invited me to present the prestigious William Belden Noble Lectures at the church during my year of leave in residence. It was a great honor and the stipend was most welcome. We received written messages expressing support from far more people than I can mention or even remember. I found special reassurance and support in the letters from those who commended me on my stand and shared with me stories of how my action had strengthened their decision to confront some authority that was blighting their lives.

Year One: Protest in Residence

The most welcome outcome of my protest has been the decision of other law schools to avoid Harvard's difficulties by stepping up their efforts to recruit and hire minority law teachers. In addition, my protest encouraged some minority lawyers to pursue teaching careers. One of them, Professor Cheryl Harris, suggests that her offer from the Chicago-Kent Law School and her acceptance in the Fall of 1990, were both influenced by my protest. She became the first woman of color to hold a tenure-line offer in the school's history.[4] Harris has developed into a fine teacher, and her first major article was published in the *Harvard Law Review*.[5] At sixty-three, I am one of the oldest minority law teachers still actively teaching. Because I was one of the first blacks to be hired at a major school, it has seemed natural to serve as the "godfather of black law teachers," a title given me several years ago at a minority law conference. My protest did not interrupt the steady stream of calls and letters I receive from other minority teachers seeking advice about teaching materials, subjects for writing, and, of course, the tenure hurdle. My responses have not gotten wiser since my protest, but those seeking my help seem to appreciate it more and follow it more often. Thus, while my protest failed to influence the Harvard faculty at which it was aimed, it has had a positive effect on a great many teachers across the country, some minority, some white. In the Fall of 1990, Professor Charles Ogletree and a student leader, Patrice Alexander Ficklin, hosted a three-day symposium supporting my protest.[6] Dozens of former students, many of them now teaching themselves, returned to Harvard for the program, which featured speeches and scholarly papers honoring my work and influence. Given the ostracism many protesters suffer, I consider myself fortunate indeed.

As for my colleagues at Harvard, most—whether or not they agreed with my protest—acted as though nothing had happened. Those opposed to my stand remained civil, while those who favored it were friendly. A few expressed concern about my financial well-being, and one faculty friend offered to pay one month of my mortgage on the strict condition that I keep his gift secret. I thanked him and promised to let him know if I needed his help. I did not fall behind in my bills, but far more than privately offered financial assistance, I needed publicly stated support for my position and active involvement in my cause.

My close friend on the faculty that year was Professor Anita Allen, a very impressive, black teacher from Georgetown Law School who the year before had accepted the Law School's offer of a year's visit. Allen had published a book and a lengthy list of law review articles and other writings. She had earned a Ph.D. in philosophy from Michigan, and when I first met her several years earlier, she was an assistant professor in the philosophy department at Carnegie-Mellon University. I, along with other black law teachers, urged Allen to consider obtaining a law degree and moving her expertise in philosophy to a law school setting. She did so, and graduated from Harvard Law School in 1984. She taught for three years at the University of Pittsburgh Law School before joining the Georgetown Law School faculty in 1987. She was awarded tenure there in 1990. Some of her writing combined law and philosophy, an interdisciplinary expertise sufficient to impress most legal scholars. While disappointed that Regina Austin had not obtained a permanent offer at Harvard, diversity advocates were optimistic about Allen. On top of her highly impressive credentials, both the faculty and the dean seemed to share the students' positive view of Allen's teaching performance.

The students recommenced their protest rallies that year and took over the dean's office on at least one occasion. When they learned of faculty meetings, they would often hold "silent vigils." Armed with hand-lettered pro-diversity signs, as many as one hundred students would line up on both sides of the door leading to the room where the faculty meeting had been scheduled. They said nothing as faculty members walked a silent gauntlet to the meeting room. When the faculty meeting ended, they reappeared in their double line. Most faculty members walked through the student lines without speaking, some voiced quiet encouragement, and a few went to ridiculous lengths to avoid the students. I continued to support all the student protest efforts as I had done in the past: speaking at the rallies, attending the coalition meetings, and trying to help the various groups negotiate their differences.

Relationships between the diverse student groups were often fragile. As with civil rights movements in the past, there were concerns that one or another of the groups was improperly dominating the Coalition's agenda. Yet despite their differences, a deep desire for greater faculty diversity was the connecting link between black, Latino, Asian, Native American student organizations and those representing women, disabled students, and gay and lesbian students. The student leader John Bonifaz says that it was "a collective sense that we could do something together" that joined the students. Walking through a major hall one morning when members of each of the Coalition groups were engaged in a sit-in by lining the walls, I could see the American melting pot in bubbling action, not amalgamating but associating, animating, becoming more than any group was separately. Here was America as it might be, and its representatives were some of our brightest and most promising young people. It seemed appropriate that these students should urge the Law School to move toward a faculty that reflected a similar spirit and strength. That they were unlikely to achieve that goal seemed suddenly far less important than their presence, working together in a cause that had already achieved another and more important goal.

In November 1990 the Coalition filed suit in a Massachusetts court against the president of Harvard and the Harvard Law School. They charged discrimination in law school faculty hiring on the basis of race, gender, ethnicity, physical disability, and sexual orientation. It was the first such suit in Harvard's history, and it reflected the commitment of the students—who did all the work in preparing and prosecuting the litigation—to assuring that the faculty would be diversified for themselves or, at least, for students who would follow them to Harvard.

At best, this suit was a long shot. In the absence of a smoking gun of intentional racial exclusion, courts are reluctant to interfere with faculty hiring and tenure processes—particularly at prestigious institutions like Harvard.[7] Among the students' claims was one I have already discussed: that by relying on criteria that had nothing to do with selecting capable law teachers but that disproportionately excluded nonwhites and non-elite whites Harvard violated the basic tenets of employment law which they were taught in their first- and second-year classes. Legal groups from across the country, organized by the Lawyers Committee for Civil Rights Under Law, and including the National Lawyers Guild, the Mexican American Legal Defense and Education Fund, the Center for Constitutional Rights, the National Conference of Black Lawyers, Lambda Legal Defense Fund, and the Society of American Law Teachers, supported the suit by filing an amicus brief on behalf of the students. The court never reached the students' substantive claims, however: it rejected the suit on technical, procedural grounds.[8] The case was appealed, and its dismissal was affirmed by Massachusetts' highest court.[9]

The courts' disappointing refusal to even hear the main issues neither surprised the students nor undermined their belief in the action. They found the case deeply satisfying. Like their other protests, the suit kept the Law School in the uncomfortable public spotlight that was most likely to force it to make the changes we all sought. Furthermore, it gave students a chance to convince Harvard of the seriousness and sincerity of their claims. Instead of pleading with Harvard just to listen to them, the students forced Harvard to defend itself. As Linda Singer, one of the student leaders, told me later, "Even though we had no doubt in our minds that we would lose the lawsuit, we felt empowered by it." She added, with a twinkle, "See, Professor Bell, you are right. Even efforts that are doomed to fail still may be worth undertaking." Or, as another of the students, Keith Boykin, said: "Even if we didn't win the case, I knew we would win."[10]

The unprecedented lawsuit filed by students against the Harvard

Year One: Protest in Residence

Law School, the students' continuing protests, and my on-leave but on-the-job presence all continued to garner media attention. Yet in spite of the pressure, law school officials successfully held to their position that they wanted more diversity on the faculty, but that their priority was merit and maintenance of the highest standards. This argument carries a weight it does not deserve, because few people understand that merit is seldom the true basis for hiring decisions. Faculties are enormously effective in using the tenure system to exclude those who, despite impressive credentials, are deemed unacceptable because of ideology, personality differences, and even more arbitrary reasons.

While faculties are quick to wrap their decision-making in the flag of academic freedom, former Yale President Kingman Brewster suggests that the greatest threat to academic freedom at major universities comes from internal pressures for intellectual conformity rather than from external interference.[11] Unfortunately, those outside the academy find it hard to believe that, as Brewster describes the "[i]ntellectual rigidity, reluctance to admit professional error, careerist jealousy, political differences, and simple personal animosity may lead committees of faculty peers to misjudge the professional work of individual colleagues."[12]

I have seen otherwise honorable faculty members engage in the most unscrupulous, underhanded conduct to avoid hiring or promoting individuals they did not wish to see admitted to their ranks. They have lied, maligned character, altered rules, manufactured precedents, and distorted policies. I am talking here about candidates for admission or tenure who are white, not minorities, candidates with impressive academic credentials, and the authors of traditional scholarly work.

When the candidate is not a white man, and either has nontraditional qualifications or departs from the traditional in scholarly subject matter and approach, the opposition can be as fierce as it is illogical and unfair. Relying on the presumption generally held by the public—and, alas, by most courts—that universities judge candidates fairly and certainly would not discriminate on the basis of race or gender, faculties unfurl the banners of merit, take their stands on the righteous ground of academic freedom, and make decisions that, however rationalized, serve to preserve those in power.

The standards for hiring and promoting faculty at Harvard Law School (and in fairness, at almost every major law school in the country) erect almost unassailable barriers of class and race. Bearing little correlation to effective teaching or significant scholarship, the criteria's most uniform effect is to produce a group of law professors whose backgrounds, education, interests, and writing most closely resemble those of the wealthy white men who have dominated law faculties since their beginning. The opportunity to obtain the necessary credentials is, we know, more readily available to those with the money, connections, and education to open the doors. To obtain each of these credentials, the candidate must excel on tests—from standardized tests like the SATs or LSATs to written essay exams—which are stacked against women and people of color. Biases inhere in every aspect of the qualification process, from college (and thus law school) admission, to course grades.[13]

Once in law school, the obstacles in the path of women and minority students do not disappear. Professor Patricia Williams has documented the way in which law school exam questions are slanted against these students. Imagine during the already daunting conditions of final exams being expected to discuss the tax implications for Kunta Kinte's owner when a slave catcher cuts off his foot; read and defend under the First Amendment a long, hateful article, "How to Be a Jew-Nigger"; or respond to a question that depicts gay men as the sole transmitters of AIDS.[14]

As a result, these barriers exclude on the basis of social class, as well as race. There are to my knowledge few, if any, white Americans on the Harvard Law School faculty whose surnames identify them as of Irish, Italian, Greek, or Polish backgrounds. There are a substantial number of Jewish professors on the faculty, but despite Harvard's once exclusionary policy toward members of that group many of its more fortunate members do not recognize that rigid adherence to standards that now favor them are any less discriminatory to others.

In my view, the almost hysterical opposition to faculty diversity is impressive proof of its need. Whatever the good faith fears of twenty years ago that outstanding grades and law review editorship earned at a major law school were absolute prerequisites for effective teaching and scholarship, they have been answered by the performance of dozens of minority (and other) law teachers who have performed well without those credentials. Yet, in spite of this, critics claim that the call for diversity reflects no more than the desire to hire less competent persons of color over intellectually gifted whites.

Again, the major opposition here is more complex than simple prejudice. The fact is, most schools *will* hire the first (though possibly not the second) black or Latino or Asian or Native American with scholastic credentials like theirs. If the minority hire holds "mainstream" ideological views, so much the better. This willingness suggests both power-preserving and community-comfort considerations, but also a culturally based (and wholly understandable—though no less misguided) desire to get beyond this nation's racial past by the simplest means possible, which is to pretend it never happened. By hiring a few token people of color—but not so many as to upset the order of things—the faculty assures itself that there is no longer an irrational, color-based barrier to the admission of blacks to the Academy. Without any earth-shattering changes in the status quo, they can promote a few people of color and then claim that things are fair and even.

But failing to deal with the underlying rules that have worked to exclude blacks from the academic enterprise, as Professor Phoebe Haddon warns, "invites grave danger: it allows us to erect a monolithic conception of competence that stifles the creative development of the discipline."[15] The standards Harvard uses to select law teachers overwhelmingly favor those who are likely to perpetuate the conventional canons of legal curricula and scholarship. Minority law teachers, particularly those of us whose writings are intended to unearth rather than entomb racial connections between past and current events, are disturbing to many whites. Many of them, seeking to rationalize their unease, tend to construe our refusal to conform as a lack of competence.

The struggle over diversity in law faculty hiring is real, not feigned. Even so, I view the compulsive focus on minority hiring as a diversionary conflict, one that is no less effective a distraction because it is perceived by so many participants on both sides as the main battle. The fact is that faculties parry the thrusts for diversity with the shield of merit, yet, when under pressure from students or alumni, law schools look beyond law school credentials and hire the best minority they can find, just as, when under pressure to cover the curriculum, they look beyond credentials and hire the best white they can find. Some of these hirees work out, some don't. The percentages of successes and failures are likely no different than for those faculty candidates so highly sought after because of their law school records, and despite their lack of either practice or teaching experience. In this case, then, the real concern is not minority diversity. Rather, law schools, like so many other institutions that adopt affirmative action policies—at least in principle—have done so to maintain intact the essential class preferences in current hiring and promotion criteria.[16]

For example, when Harvard discovered Scott Brewer, a black who was the editor-in-chief of the *Yale Law Journal* and an outstanding student, they acted with as much speed and enthusiasm as anyone—including this critic—could ask. Following graduation from law school, Brewer needed a final year to complete his work on a Ph.D. in philosophy. The Law School invited him to Cambridge and gave him an office and a stipend to teach a jurisprudence course even before he gained his degree. Scott was treated as a junior faculty person and impressed everyone with his scholarly potential. Before the end of the year, the faculty voted him an assistant professorship. They made the offer knowing that it would be two years until he completed already arranged judicial clerkships on the court of appeals and the Supreme Court and could join the faculty. When during the faculty discussion, someone asked the Appointments Committee whether the Yale Law School was planning to offer Brewer a position, the answer was, "We don't know and we don't care. Let's vote." They did.

For at bottom, Harvard—and most other law school faculties—simply resist restructuring the hiring and promotion requirements to bring them into line with laws that would require the school to prove that the stated job qualifications for a professorship reasonably relate to the skills required for the position.[17] Of course, revamping law school hiring procedures might bring in some of the extremely successful practitioners who now, despite their achievements as lawyers, can't get serious consideration from many law schools unless they have done extremely well in law school. It might result in the hiring of more white Americans from ethnic groups that are now virtually absent from Harvard's faculty ranks.

It is heresy, but I think really good law teachers are made and not simply born. Law teachers should have extensive experience practicing law, and want both to train law students and to write about their views on law which have come out of their practice and training. But in hiring and promoting few law schools give priority to these experiences. As for predicting teaching ability, outstanding grades are as likely to signal undeveloped social skills as they are the interactional capability good teachers should possess. Empathy, an essential teaching trait, is often found in people for whom law study was a challenge rather than in those who easily earned high grades. Minority status does not guarantee excellence in teaching or anything else; but subordinate status brings with it an understanding of the society and those who run it that is certainly unique and worth sharing with students and colleagues.

Far from conflicting, the goals of diversity and academic freedom and excellence should converge. The current controversy reflects the contradictory allegiances of those who invoke and exercise their academic freedom to exclude those who are not like them either in background or ideology. The preservation of this academic nepotism and ideological uniformity is the hidden agenda of far too many law faculty members. It is a stance that unjustly excludes those who would be the worthy teachers our students want and need.

In the Spring of 1991, as the first anniversary of my protest leave approached, I decided to accept an invitation for a year's visit from New York University Law School's dean, John Sexton. By then, it was apparent that those Harvard faculty members who differed with me regarding the value of faculty diversity certainly were not moved to change their views by either my presence in protest or student activism. Many students beseeched me, in individual letters and lengthy petitions, to remain and continue the fight at Harvard for a second year. I interpreted their messages of good will as both an acknowledgment of what I had done and a commitment on their part to continue in my absence. Sadly, but with hope that the diversity advocates would continue their work, I left for New York.

FIVE

Year Two:
Protest in Exile

The Council of Elders debated long and passionately about how to resolve the lowlanders' revolt. Finally, it was Xercis' moment to speak. As he moved from his chair to the center of the podium, he looked suddenly old, weighed by his sixty years.

"I am drawn to both sides of this debate. To you who advocate armed resistance—but I fear that a victory bought with great bloodshed will surely foment even more fierce revolt. To you who urge patience—but inaction can be seen as weakness and will only encourage the rebels." He paused, then went on. "In this dilemma, I suggest a third course.

"Let us tell the lowlanders that we have always intended one day to provide them with representation at the Citadel. That this day has now come. That we will open up the Citadel to them." As the Elders started to mutter angrily, Xercis raised his hand for silence. "At the same time, we must warn them that their presence here"—he looked around the great Council chamber—"will meet resistance from some members of the Citadel and from some lowlanders as well. Thus, change must be gradual, building support and acceptance as it proceeds." He paused.

Many among the Council thought that Xercis had suffered a serious attack of senility. For the first time in Xercis' rule, the Elders interrupted him and openly questioned his decision. "Admitting a low-

lander," one cried, "is surrender." Added another: "Surrender, yes, but without its dignity!" Two or three Elders discerned the outlines of Xercis' strategy. "Allow him to finish," they interjected. "We must not forget that the most potent weapon in the arsenal of power is not brute force, but guile."

"We can in one action," Xercis went on, "assuage the rage of the lowlanders while making it appear that fate, rather than ourselves, is the source of the conditions about which they complain. By admitting a few of them slowly, we will appear fair and open-minded. We will win the allegiance of those who enter the Citadel, and quell the complaints of those who say we exclude lowlanders from our ranks. Those who join us will praise the qualities that earned their entry to the Citadel. Those who remain outside will blame the personal shortcomings that keep them below. Most lowlanders, meanwhile, if they respond as they have in the past, will blame their exclusion from the Citadel on the radicals among them who foment distrust with demands for preferential treatment and percentages of representation. The majority will not join the revolt.

"We will win," Xercis concluded, "by admitting the error of our past policies. Only by ostensibly renouncing them, will we ensure their continued viability." Though he did not mention her name, Xercis realized that he had learned something from Tamar—though perhaps not the lesson she most wished to convey. After long and often bitter debate, Xercis gained the Council's approval for his plan. The Citadel would admit one lowlander to the Council, provided the individual was of their choosing.

When I moved to New York City in August of 1991 to begin my visit at the N.Y.U. Law School, I leased my Cambridge townhouse with a reasonable expectation that I would return to Harvard the following year. As events were to prove, my optimism was misplaced. While the Appointments Committee justified Austin's rejection by pointing to what they regarded as unimpressive credentials

Year Two: Protest in Exile

and unscholarly work, Anita Allen, the black visitor the year before from Georgetown, seemed to satisfy their craving for superior credentials. Allen's educational background and publication record was superior to that of a good number of faculty members. Allen's scholarship, moreover, is more traditional and less controversial and probably appealed to a larger segment of the faculty than did Austin's work. Allen's book, *Uneasy Access*, for example, focuses on privacy rights from a feminist perspective, but it is filled with legal citations and contains an impressive discussion of philosophical and doctrinal issues which should have satisfied even the most pedantic faculty members.[1]

Early in the Fall, prior to the Appointments Committee's negative recommendation on Austin, it became obvious that many faculty members—with good and bad intentions—were playing Allen and Austin against each other. The majority of the faculty who did not support Austin avoided criticism by promising to be more supportive of Anita Allen. Professors who might otherwise have voted for Austin agreed, either on their own initiative or at the request of other faculty members, to avoid making Austin's tenure an issue and bank the good will they earned to spend on Allen's more viable bid.

I found this mostly unspoken process frustrating. Its underlying assumption, was, of course, that there was only one position for a black woman on the Law School's faculty. Thus, consciously or not, the faculty could move into a mode familiar to all minority law teachers: deferring each current candidate for the more promising one in the pipeline. As each candidate came up for consideration, she was rejected or tabled in favor of someone who—never having suffered the bruising and microscopic examination of a Harvard visit—was more appealing than the candidate at hand. At least one faculty member, in parrying my question about how he felt about Allen, responded, "She's o.k., but I gather the Appointments Committee may be thinking of extending a visit to Lani Guinier, a University of Pennsylvania Law professor with more practice experience than either

Austin or Allen." I simply looked at him. He and I both knew that experience in law practice is low on the list of qualifications for Harvard's law faculty and that a substantial number of Harvard's faculty have little or none.

Despite Allen's obvious and traditional qualifications for a tenured position, and a very productive visit, she fared no better than Austin. Her treatment—particularly given the fact that she had been almost unanimously cited in discussions about Austin as the exemplar of a qualified candidate—only highlighted the faculty's unwillingness to act in the absence of pressures greater than Coalition students and I were able to generate.

Dean Clark, on a number of occasions, praised Allen's work during her visit, and promised that her name would be brought to the faculty early in the 1991–92 school year. But by late Fall, Allen had not heard from the dean. Indeed, after returning to Georgetown, Allen's main contact with the law school administration was through Professor Randall Kennedy, a young, black professor who had been appointed to the all-important Appointments Committee as soon as he gained tenure in 1989. Kennedy had not supported Regina Austin, but he was enthusiastic about Allen. One would have hoped, and I think Kennedy expected, that his willingness to vote against Austin— "really courageous," one professor called it—would give weight to his support for Allen. Moreover, while Harvard could point to Kennedy's stand on Austin as proof that their rejection of her was not racially motivated, they would have no similar shield if they voted Allen down.

Kennedy told me in December of 1991 that he planned to "walk the halls" visiting faculty offices to campaign on Allen's behalf. Kennedy, though, underestimated the faculty's virulent ideological struggle, which would take priority over diversity concerns. Faculty candidates whose work or interests fell into the liberal camp were anathema to the conservative camp. The liberals, who had voted for several conservative candidates in recent years in the expectation— always disappointed—that conservatives would return the favor and support liberal applicants, were determined not to make the same mistake again. As a result, appointments of any kind were extremely difficult to make.

In late February 1992 the faculty worked out a compromise to satisfy its warring factions and to remove the barriers that had virtually deadlocked the appointments process. Each side would select three candidates whom they wanted to hire *and* who would be acceptable to the other side. As I understand it, Anita Allen's name was on the liberal list, but when several middle-of-the road faculty members announced that they would not support one of the three conservative candidates, his name, despite the outrage of some of the conservative faculty members, was dropped. To prevent the whole deal from falling through, the liberals had to drop one of their candidates. Evidently, while they supported Allen, the left-liberals did not consider her "one of them." When the final appointments deal was approved, Allen's name was not on it. All those hired were white men.

I imagine the explanations for what happened are as numerous as the faculty members who approved the deal. Interestingly enough, though, the political compromise was only acceptable because it seemed to the participants to involve ideology and not race. Just imagine if diversity supporters proposed to accept two white candidates if two minority candidates were tenured. Opponents of affirmative action would have roared their horror. Because the deal that resulted in tenure for four white males, who became known as the "gang of four," fit the faculty members' personal interests in bringing into their ranks others like them and appeared to involve politics, not race, it was deemed an honorable compromise.

It has always astounded me—perhaps more than it should—that white people willing to accept so much unfairness in admissions and job programs inevitably and vehemently draw the line when that unfairness seems to derive from racial or gender preference. For all of the litigation and self-righteous rhetoric that stems from opposition to programs that favor women and minorities, I have not heard of white protests against the widespread policies that favor people on the basis of wealth or social status. Where are the lawsuits challenging preferences either for alumnae or geographic region in college admissions, or against graduate school criteria that favor graduates of elite and expensive undergraduate schools? Even though the children of Harvard alumnae can point to no history of slavery or other class-based discrimination, no one questions their entitlement to special treatment in Harvard admissions.

Some years ago, I spent a day lecturing at Pace University Law School in Westchester County. In speaking to various classes and in the question and answer period following a school-wide lecture, I noted a quite strong opposition to affirmative action programs. One articulate white student acknowledged the discrimination blacks had suffered in the past. "Now, though, everyone must make it on merit. That is the American way." In response, I suggested to him that while he seemed quite able, as able as the students I had taught at Harvard and met at Yale and Columbia Law Schools, when he graduated from Pace he would have a hard time competing at large corporate law firms, whose hiring partners prefer to hire lawyers whose parents had been able to send them to Harvard, Yale, and Columbia. "What," I asked him, "do you have to say about that?" He paused, eyes glazed. Obviously, he was so focused on what he called "reverse discrimination" that he had not thought about the possibility of his being passed by for jobs because he had not come from an upper-class background.

"That's the breaks," he said finally. I looked at him in wonder. "In other words," I said, "you will be deeply suspicious if any black—no matter how able—gets a job you want, but you will step aside and let upper-class whites no smarter than you take jobs you want to advance your career and support your family?" "Well," he said finally, trying to muster a degree of dignity, "one of these days, I hope to be able to send my kids to Harvard and Yale." I shook my head. Racism has been devastating to blacks, but it has also done serious harm to a great many whites.

Year Two: Protest in Exile

Paradoxically, or more accurately, hypocritically, three of the four white men who obtained permanent appointments under the "gang of four" package deal were visitors during the school year when they were appointed. Evidently, the faculty's refusal to consider visitors for tenure during the year of their visits was not considered an obstacle to those appointments. It did not seem to matter that over the past two years, the Law School had repeatedly refused students' and my own requests to waive that rule for minority candidates. The rule was specifically invoked both in campus discussions and with the media to justify delaying action on Austin and Allen's appointments. Over the prior decade, at least three other minority visitors were told that, because of the rule, no faculty action could be taken to consider them for permanent positions during the year of their visits. In several instances, negative student evaluations were later given as reasons why no tenure offer had been forthcoming. The newly tenured white visitors did not have to undergo student evaluations.

When confronted by students about this blatant disregard of the school's policy, Dean Clark first denied that there was any such policy. Then, he issued a memo in which he claimed that the appointment of these four visitors did not violate the year-away policy because that policy had been rescinded before their tenure decisions.[2] Asked why he did not notify students of a change in a policy they had so loudly contested, Clark claimed that he did not know they would be interested in such a detail. Apparently, he did not think that President Rudenstine would be interested either, since Rudenstine was quoted by the press as saying that he was not told that the year-away rule had been rescinded.[3] In his memo, Clark wrote that a new rule had been adopted, allowing visitors to be considered during the term of their visit when "institutional needs and practical considerations are judged to justify doing so." According to the dean, the year-away rule was revoked before Anita Allen and Gerald Torres—a Latino professor from the University of Minnesota who visited at Harvard the same year as Professor Allen—finished their visits, yet faculty indifference or hostility still stalled evaluation of both of their candidacies. To add insult to injury, the faculty then adopted a resolution urging the Appointments Committee to consider by the Fall of 1992 several promising candidates who were not white males (almost identical to the one, described earlier, which the faculty adopted a full decade earlier, in 1982).

Whatever its value in breaking the faculty stalemate, the selection of faculty candidates by political trade-off shows that the school's proclaimed determination to hire "strictly based on merit" was little more than convenient, self-deceiving rhetoric. Notably, unlike the fierce outcry raised by those who claimed that hiring diverse candidates insulted their commitment-to-merit norms, I understand that not a single faculty member dissented from this deal.

Alienation, far more than anger or disappointment, best describes my reaction to the faculty hiring decisions. Even in New York, far from the scene, I felt a profound sense of rejection. My feeling was not lessened by the faculty's likely insistence that their action had nothing to do with me or other blacks on the faculty. And it is true that the thick layers of elitism at the Law School create an atmosphere that is alienating to all. I remember receiving a handwritten letter from Professor Archibald Cox in 1974 after I had notified Dean Sacks that it was my last year as the only black faculty member. Cox, who seemed to me the archetypal Harvard Law faculty member, urged me to remain and not confuse my failure to get faculty action on more minority hiring with the aloof and distant atmosphere of the place. In all his years there, Cox confessed, he never felt anyone at Harvard gave a damn about him. I have always appreciated that insight into the school, written—as it were—from the other side.

Later in the Spring of my second protest year, many of my friends on the Harvard faculty spoke out against an outrageous parody written by students for a law school publication. Their action came in response to a terrible tragedy, the murder near her Cambridge home of Mary Jo Frug, a New England Law School professor, a feminist legal scholar, and the wife of the Harvard law professor Gerald Frug.

Year Two: Protest in Exile

Exactly one year after her murder, the *Harvard Law Review* published for its annual banquet a satirical magazine, the *Harvard Law Revue*, which contained an unspeakably cruel parody of Professor Frug and her writings. The article, which made national news and sparked another major controversy involving Harvard, galvanized many faculty members, including some who up until then had been silent on the diversity issue. The tasteless parody finally made them recognize what my protest apparently did not: that the Law School had created an elitist environment indifferent to human feelings. Fifteen faculty members signed a letter soundly criticizing the Law School:

> Harvard Law School has done far too little to address issues of sexism and misogyny. It has sustained an environment pervaded by these attitudes, while failing to take the actions required to transform that environment. A central factor in that hostile environment is a faculty whose composition, and whose processes of self-replication, profoundly undervalue the contributions that a more genuinely diverse group of teachers and scholars could make.
>
> It is simply wrong to suppose that greater diversity among us—diversity in a sense deeper than is represented by a judicious ideological mix—could be purchased only be sacrificing intellectual and legal excellence. We are sometimes prone to foolishness, hypocrisy, and self-deception in our judgments of scholarly work, and our unthinking acceptance of what is more familiar to us.
>
> We know that many of our colleagues think it is mistaken to draw a connection between the grotesque violation of Mary Jo Frug's life and death and the nature and priorities of this institution, including its hiring practices. But we are convinced that failure to see this connection is itself a significant part of the problem.[4]

The letter marked, as Professor Laurence Tribe said, "the first time that a significant number of the faculty have collectively criticized the institution as a whole," and received a great deal of media attention.[5] I thought it a fine statement, and true, although I was struck that it pointedly failed to mention the diversity protests that had been making the same points for years.

The feminist legal scholar Catherine MacKinnon is supposed to have said that plagiarism, far from being a rip-off, is the sincerest form of flattery. This observation is likely the only acknowledgment protesters will receive from either those in authority or some of those who share their views. Even so, there is the gnawing question: what would the students and I have had to do to spark a similarly strong public statement from the faculty members who signed the letter condemning the Mary Jo Frug travesty? They obviously—and, I think, correctly—saw the lack of diversity as a contributing cause of the incident. Many of the signers are long-time friends who shared my views and regretted my loss. And yet, for whatever reasons, they did not link my diversity protest with their charge that lack of diversity had set a climate for the cruel parody.

About that time, Professor Roger Fisher wrote me expressing the view that the appointments by slate set a precedent that minority candidates would be able to benefit from in the future. He felt that the resolution urging a stepped-up search for minorities would bring positive results. Fisher's letter served as a reminder that I would soon have to decide whether to return to Harvard, despite its failure to make any progress on diversity issues, or seek to extend my protest leave for a third year. I gave the matter a great deal of thought and summarized those thoughts in my response.

"Try as I may," I wrote him, "I can't share your optimism," because on too many occasions I had relied on administration promises to diversify the faculty, only to see minority candidates—or most of them—rejected and more white males hired. Fisher had expressed concern that the school would not extend my leave and that my continued protest could alienate faculty and thus jeopardize my chance for reappointment. I thanked him for his concern, but reiterated the belief that my protest was a necessary step to reform hiring and promotion policies that, in their present form, so denigrate my accomplishments—achieved without the academic credentials the faculty deems so important—and so diminishes the worth of my position in hiring and promoting faculty, that I could not return even if my continued absence doomed any chance of reappointment.

Roger Fisher, a good friend over the years, was expressing his personal concern, but as a skilled negotiator who had tried without success to work out an accommodation that would have made my protest unnecessary, he likely had the dean's approval for his letter. The appeal process lay ahead, but the handwriting was on the wall. Unless other faculty members who supported more diversity in the hiring process bestirred themselves, my tenure at Harvard would soon come to an end.

SIX

The Expulsion

The host of lowlanders moved the line of their blockade close to the Citadel's walls. They expected that their clamor for social reform and representation would bring the Citadel's rulers rushing to the ramparts. Instead, the gates swung open, and the Citadel's leaders came forth and called for a small delegation of lowlanders to meet with them.

Xercis was distressed but not surprised to see Tamar in the lowlanders' delegation. She had quietly left the Citadel some weeks before, leaving only a sealed letter for him. "Dear Father, I have decided to work for the Citadel's future among the least of its peoples. Living close to them, I will be able to assess their needs and evaluate how the Citadel's rulers can best respond to them. I realize that my absence can jeopardize my chances of succeeding you, and may even provide an opportunity for my opponents to expel me from the Citadel. I accept these risks. I will always consider the Citadel my home, and I will always deserve my place there." As she predicted, many of the Citadel's Elders did deem his daughter's desertion an act of treason. Her departure was a heavy blow to Xercis, and now he did not greet her.

As Tamar stepped forward to speak for the lowlanders, Xercis raised his hand. "Let me speak, Tamar. When you have heard the Council's decision in this matter, we will hear from you." His voice rang out,

93

stilling the crowd. "For years we—the Elders and I—have allowed no lowlander to serve in the Council of Elders. Now, you have made us realize that this is intolerable. We have come to understand that you should be a part of the Citadel, and we are prepared to welcome you. But in all of our best interests, we must lay down guidelines for this historic transition."

His words stunned the crowd into silence, as he continued. "Governing our vast domain is a difficult and exacting task. Not everyone is able to rise to its demands, and we must not, as a nation, risk elevating anyone who lacks the skill and wisdom to do so. Therefore, we will admit to the Citadel only those lowlanders who meet our time-honored qualifications."

The delegation conferred. To most of them, it seemed an honor to have admission to the Council be based on merit. With great solemnity and joy, they accepted Xercis' proposal. After agreeing that an open competition would be held on a set date, the delegation promised to suspend the blockade. As they left the Citadel, every lowlander in the delegation believed that its walls had moved, if only a little. So Tamar believed as well, and she returned to the Citadel with her father.

My request that in my case the University waive its rule limiting faculty leaves to two years met with no more success than any of my previous efforts to get Harvard to change the way it does business. When I refused to return to the Law School for what would be the third year of my protest, citing Harvard's continued failure to hire a woman of color, I was fired. After sixteen years on the faculty, my career at Harvard was ended.

Let me be clear. I do not contend that Harvard University's rule limiting leaves of absence to two years was written with a racially discriminatory purpose. Rather, I argued that the rule was intended for other situations, to discourage faculty from remaining away from the University for long periods while pursuing other and—for them—more interesting or profitable aspects of their careers. It almost certainly was not designed to frustrate conscience-based protests like mine.

In fact, the rule in practice is meaningless. Faculty members simply resign when their activities away from Harvard render inconvenient a return after two years. They do so in the almost certain knowledge that on completion of their duties their school will vote them a new appointment. This, of course, was my experience when I resigned the Oregon deanship. The law faculty voted me a new appointment. Now, of course, as Professor Roger Fisher and other faculty friends had made clear, my protest had upset a number of faculty members, and a new appointment, were I to seek it, would be far from guaranteed.

Having said that, I believe that when first Dean Clark, and then the new university president, Neil Rudenstine, invoked the two-year leave limit to bar my request for a third year of leave, they did so in full expectation that its implementation would force me to end my protest and return to Harvard. Because none of them could imagine leaving Harvard for any reason, they could not conceive that I might refuse to return if the loss of my position would be the price of continuing to adhere to my principles.

In correspondence with Dean Clark, I acknowledged the regulation, but asserted that the rule was intended for faculty members who wished to remain for long periods of time in government positions or other prestigious posts. The rule, I argued, should not serve as a barrier to the continuation of my leave protesting faculty practices that elevate credentialism over competence. Reminding him of my twenty-year commitment to increasing the number of minority faculty, I wrote that my conscience required that I seek to convey convictions through my protest that he and the faculty ignored when I expressed them orally and in writing. I contended that, as they pertain to minorities in general, and to women of color in particular, the faculty's hiring and promotion practices are in violation of both University affirmative action rules and possibly state and federal law as well. Whether legal or not, the policies I contested served to deny me my entitlement to work in an academic community where diversity of race, gender, background, and experience is not severely circumscribed by hiring practices that exclude many potentially fine teachers and scholars—including most black and other minority candidates.

Dean Clark rejected my argument and advised that my failure to report my intention to return would result in the termination of my tenured position. Because there was no established appeal process, I asked Professor Frank Michelman to prepare a letter to Harvard President Neil Rudenstine that could serve as background for a face-to-face meeting. Frank did so, pointing out the uniqueness of my request for a third year of leave. He noted Harvard's written commitment to affirmative action hiring and the importance of my efforts to carrying out that commitment. Rudenstine, in a response obviously honed by the University's lawyers, ignored our request for a meeting, treated the letter as an appeal, and denied it. Michelman was deeply upset by the President's refusal to extend the basic courtesy of a meeting to a tenured faculty member. I was disappointed, but also amused—as blacks are from time to time—when we recognize how easy it is to frighten whites, notwithstanding the fact that they hold all the power.

I sought to take the case to Harvard's governing boards, the Corporation and the Board of Overseers. Advised that most board members were away for the summer, I suggested that we postpone the hearing until the Fall when both the board members and the students would be back on campus. This definitely was not acceptable. The University did not relish a hearing at which students might mount protests. Instead, the president's office arranged for a small group of members of the Corporation and the Board of Overseers to meet with me in late July. The appeal was scheduled at 17 Quincy Street, the former university president's residence. Ironically, this was the same building that, in my fictional protest story, was mysteriously blown up, killing the university president and all the black faculty

The Expulsion

members and finally inspiring the school to launch a major effort to recruit minority candidates.[1] Perhaps University officials remembered my story, for on the morning of the hearing, uniformed and plainclothes security personnel were visibly present around the building.

The hearing committee was chaired by Professor Henry Rosovsky, a long-time Harvard stalwart, and included four or five other prestigious members of the Corporation or the Board of Overseers. Harvard had also invited one black woman, Boston College law professor Renee Landers, a first-year member of the Board of Overseers. Despite what must have been the discomfort of her role, Professor Landers asked pertinent questions and made sensitive comments. After receiving a letter from the Board rejecting my appeal, I wrote Professor Landers and, in addition to thanking her for her efforts, expressed my regret that those who organized the meeting placed her in a most unenviable position. As the only minority and the only woman in attendance, she was rather obviously present to give the proceeding a semblance of legitimacy without regard to our dignity or concern about their civility.

Harvard's higher boards were not likely to reverse the decision of a president they had installed only a year before. Even so, Frank Michelman and I diligently pressed the appeal. I reviewed the history of efforts to increase the presence of minorities at Harvard. My leave, I contended, was to protest what I considered the Law School's failure to keep the bargain it made when I was hired. The board members were cordial, but not moved. Some weeks later, I received the formal notice rejecting my appeal. My tenure at the Harvard Law School was over.

There was a measure of humor in this defeat. In retrospect, I think President Rudenstine was right in his claim that he would not be able to administer the two-year leave limitation rule if he made an exception for acts of conscience. I was certainly right in arguing that my career of using protest to bring about racial reform in Harvard and elsewhere justified an exception. After all, as I declared in my statement, over the years, to paraphrase Shakespeare's Othello, "I have done the state some service. And they know it." Recognizing an exception to a rule never intended to cover a situation like mine was an action Harvard might have taken to acknowledge my efforts to achieve the racial inclusiveness about which they like to boast.

But if President Rudenstine actually meant that by granting an exception for me, a black involved in a civil rights protest against the University, he could not, given political reality, deny a similar extension to a prestigious white professor, even if it was sought on the flimsiest excuse, then I must agree that he is right. I can easily imagine the indignation of Harvard's "best and brightest" upon their extended leave requests being rejected in the wake of Derrick Bell's extension having been granted.

This no-win dilemma is not only almost farcical, but also tragically prophetic in its similarity to the racial barriers white society has so carefully constructed that are at least as disabling to whites as they are to blacks. For, of course, a rule without exceptions is an instrument capable of doing mischief to the innocent and bringing grief—as well as injustice—to those who should gain exemptions from the rule's functioning. Surely, it takes no great leap of imagination to think of individuals involved in research or other projects both vital to the institution or to the society and sufficiently unpopular with their faculty colleagues to make extension of leaves imperative if they are to keep their jobs. President Rudenstine, or his successors, having denied my leave request on grounds that appeared bizarre to many, will likely have little difficulty in distinguishing my case from any of these. But the price of such tortured distinctions will be a further loss of Harvard's reputation as a place where those in charge operate with good sense, to say nothing of a concern for simple justice.

Another irony is that it would have been easy enough for Harvard to accommodate me and avoid violating its stated policy at the same time—had the school wanted to do so. At the hearing, I mentioned that, as a technical matter, the two-year rule should not apply to me. In the first year of my protest, while not on the payroll, I had remained at the school, handled many of my duties, and taught a course. Without any difficulty under these circumstances, the President or Board of Overseers could have held that the first year of my protest would not count towards the leave limit and extended my tenure for another year. The school would have gained an additional year to try to deal with the underlying diversity crisis and avoided the issue entirely if it hired a woman of color during that time. Had the University had any intention of making a tenure offer to a woman of color within the near future, this would have been the obvious course of action. However, the University never proposed this strategy, and I never asked them to.

Had the case involved a professor whom they really did not wish to lose, the University would certainly have found some strategy that would have avoided the draconian result in my case. The problem, quite simply, is that to the people applying the rules, the interests and values of blacks and other outsiders seldom merit priority in the absence of a crisis or when nonrecognition of such interests is cost free. When the Law School's overwhelmingly white male faculty became convinced that a supposedly ideologically balanced slate was the only way to make additions to the faculty, they forged ahead and found their solution in slate hiring. Yet, despite their frequently voiced commitment to faculty diversity, no one in this process was willing to hold out for the inclusion of one minority woman. With their *own* personal interests at stake—in this case, the hiring of candidates with beliefs like their own (and one could easily imagine a time and place where skin color or gender was the deciding factor)—blacks were, quite literally, traded away in the bargain. Just as one could imagine a different end to the story of faculty diversity, one can imagine a different end to the decision to terminate my tenure if those charged with deciding my fate, again, cared deeply about the issue of racial inclusion at the Law School. But as long as those deciding when and

CONFRONTING AUTHORITY

how to apply the rules feel no real loyalty to the needs of blacks and other minority groups, we blacks will continue to find ourselves always on the wrong end of the rule. Under such circumstances, the mounting of protests is more than a political option, it is a moral imperative.

SEVEN

Silent Acquiescence: The Too-High Price of Prestige

In the weeks following the Citadel's offer, the lowlanders diligently prepared for the competition that would grant one of them a seat on the Council of Elders. The aspirants were to respond orally to a series of questions designed to test their leadership ability. Xercis and the Elders would evaluate their answers and choose the most impressive person to fill the first (and only) available seat on the Council of Elders.

As they listened to the competing lowlanders, the Elders were wary. Although they had agreed to the competition, they had not accepted that any lowlander would be their equal. Although many of the competitors answered correctly the complex questions the Elders had labored to devise, the expertise of one young man amazed them. Indeed, this Timur demolished most of their serious reservations about admitting a lowlander. Even when his answers were identical to the other contestants', he still outshone them.

He also had, for a lowlander, a distinguished pedigree, and his family had managed to accumulate an unusual amount of wealth. They had invested their money in Timur's future, sending him to a superior school in another land, a school that, unlike the best schools in their kingdom, admitted lowlanders. There, Timur had excelled and cul-

tivated many of the qualities shared by those in the Citadel. He under-stood several now-obsolete languages which allowed him to study ob-scure historical texts. He also had joined exclusive fraternities, known for their allegiance to pursuing "the best in life." Many of the friends he made, the children of the elite in other kingdoms, spoke highly of him to their counterparts in the Citadel. You could almost forget, they noted in praise, that Timur was a lowlander.

In addition, Timur was different in his manner from the other low-lander competitors. He lacked the brash assertiveness of those who felt entitled to join the Citadel. Nor was he timid, like the lowlanders who seemed to possess no self-confidence after years of being ignored, dis-missed, and placed in jobs below their abilities. Timur answered all questions confidently but respectfully—even cheerfully. Thus, finding the delicate balance admired by the Elders, he did not appear threat-ening. If they closed their eyes and heard only his soft voice, they might think he was one of them.

Xercis observed the Elders nod in approval when Timur spoke. The other competing lowlanders noticed as well. Some grew angry and openly challenged the Elders—an obvious mistake. Others, thoroughly flustered, misspoke when called upon.

At the close of the competition, the winner was clear to all. Xercis made the announcement: "We have seen today that a break in our hallowed traditions need not invite disaster. Timur has done well for himself. He is truly a credit to his race and should be accepted as their representative into the Council of Elders. I so move." The vote was unanimous. Even those who had harbored misgivings accepted Timur without reservation.

Xercis continued: "I must also add that we owe much of today's events to my daughter, Tamar." And to allay the concern and resent-ment Tamar had caused by taking on the lowlanders' cause, he said: "Tamar's willingness to go out among the people, to observe their distress, and to recognize their potential moved us to this event and convince us that our beloved Citadel will be able to adapt to the chal-lenges of the future, as we and our predecessors have met them in the past."

There is a sense in which mounting a protest is like crossing the border into a foreign and not very friendly country. You find yourself suddenly speaking a different language, one that the natives neither understand nor care to have translated. The natives are people you know but who, somehow, now don't care to know you. They certainly do not wish to identify with your protest. Strange. If you are successful, they too will benefit, but they seem to see only the risks that may envelop them unless they keep their distance and—if necessary—disown this stranger who was once an old friend, a valued work associate, one of them. The protester's inability to communicate renders it impossible even to discuss, much less convince associates of, the positive, self-affirming value of confronting authority.

At one point during my protest leave, Professor Christopher Edley, a former student and now a Harvard Law faculty member, took me aside and said, "Derrick, I agree with your goals, but I don't agree with your tactics." Coming from Chris, one of the Law School's most outspoken faculty critics, this support-in-part seemed strange. What I think he meant was that I should return to the school and fight from within. More than most, Chris never failed to make clear to me his feeling that my presence was an asset greater than anything I hoped to accomplish by my absence. A public confrontation, though, seemed to him, and to many of the faculty, beyond the rules, a form of academic unsportsmanlike conduct.

While their reasons differed, most of the Harvard faculty who supported greater diversity in concept fell into the "agreement with goals, but not tactics" camp. Professor Duncan Kennedy, a leader of the Critical Legal Studies movement, said as much. Often referred to as CRITS, CLS adherents challenged the sacred orthodoxy that the law has a neutral and fixed meaning. Duke Professor Stanley Fish describes the group as "a left-leaning segment of the legal academy whose members argue that legal reasoning is not a formal mechanism for determining outcomes in a neutral fashion—as traditional legal scholars maintain—but is rather a ramshackle ad hoc affair whose ill-fitting joints are soldered together by suspect rhetorical gestures, leaps of illogic, and special pleadings tricked up as general rules, all in the service of a decidedly partisan agenda that wants to wrap itself in the mantle and majesty of THE LAW."[1]

Each year, CLS supporters held a meeting to explain the ideology to incoming students. While not a member of the group, I was usually invited to speak and discuss developments in the somewhat similar critical race theory. Accepting such an invitation during the last year of my in-residence protest, I, along with three or four CLS adherents, presented a short talk. During the question and answer period, a black student, noting the CLS faculty members' stated commitment to social reform, asked what they were doing to support my protest. There was an embarrassed silence and a great deal of foot shuffling at the front of the room. Finally, Duncan Kennedy went to the microphone and pointed out that he was on leave that year. The groans from the audience reflected their displeasure with that explanation. Then Kennedy explained—forthrightly, I thought—that he respected the action I had taken, but that it was simply not his way of bringing about change.

Duncan Kennedy speaks for the majority of academics. But why? These individuals hold some of the most secure and comfortable positions this society has to offer. They have, as Franklin Delano Roosevelt elegantly put it, "nothing to fear but fear itself." Fear, though, can be a many-splendored specter. Consider the dialogue in John Kenneth Galbraith's novel *A Tenured Professor*, in which a promising graduate student expresses his intention to become an economist and to further liberal causes, working for peace, the poor, the inner cities, and greater equality in income distribution.[2] A senior professor warns him his plans are unwise and impractical and will ensure that he will not get tenure:

> Tenure was originally invented to protect radical professors, those who challenged the accepted order. But we don't have such people anymore at the universities, and the reason *is* tenure.

When the time comes to grant it nowadays, the radicals get screened out. That's its principal function. It's a very good system, really—keeps academic life at a decent level of tranquility.

In response to the graduate student's suggestion that perhaps he will wait until he gains tenure to express his liberal tendencies, the professor agrees that this is the only sensible choice. But he warns that "by then conformity will be a habit. You'll no longer be a threat to the peace and comfort of our ivied walls. The system really works."

Professor Gerald Frug offers an explanation that is probably more palatable to passive scholars. In a long article, he seeks to distinguish the motivations of the academic from those of the activist.[3] Academics, he suggests, are intellectual puritans, working in purposeful and solitary shelter. They believe, as a matter of faith, that pure thought, free of instrumental considerations, will flourish of its own inherent logic. Strong, determined action taken to advance their ideas not only sullies these ideas, but undermines their transformative power. Thus, while the academic can "persuade"—demonstrating the moral and intellectual soundness of their philosophy—they cannot "pressure" others to adopt or act upon their ideas.

> This is not just a matter of tactics; it is not right to pressure people into changing their views. In making moral judgments of this kind, academics defend themselves by advancing a moral principle to which they can adhere; as academics, their position would be weakened if there were not some principled way to defend their actions against critics.

Where academics disdain action, Frug argues that activists thrive upon it:

> They view inaction not as a sign of prudent self-protection but as a sign of inadequacy, a sign that they have no useful contribution to make. Far from wanting to escape from the dangers of political involvement, activists pride themselves on their will-

ingness to make an effort to influence local, national, even international, events. Of course, activists realize that any course of action they choose to take will have its problems. But they tend to fear more that their actions won't be strong enough than that their actions will be too strong to be justified.

Instrumentalism, which the academic sees as unprincipled and anti-intellectual, sets the activist's course. To the activist "[i]mmorality derives less from failure of principle than from weakness and self-doubt. Activists acknowledge that they cannot involve themselves in every case of injustice, but, on those that count, they must do what they can for what they believe."[4]

Frug's statement of the issue is persuasive, and, to my mind, it explains—but does not exonerate—the academic who is satisfied with things as they are, or who views social evils only as subjects for study and debate. The academic who admits that his or her role is that of a social critic, not a social reformer, at least honestly assumes the function of a theorist. Academics who claim that, simply by writing about the need for change, they are fighting to make that change set a standard for judging themselves which they will not and cannot meet. Almost by definition, Critical Legal Studies adherents are committed to both uncover and reform social evils. Academic activity alone, though, will neither move those in power nor create the groundswell that will force those in power to move. Indeed, even effective intellectual effort requires active involvement. It is inconceivable that Dr. King could have so powerfully conveyed his frustrations and defended his struggle in his Letter from a Birmingham Jail had he not composed that letter in prison—literally on the field of battle.

I saw the deficiencies in Professor Frug's theory played out in the Law School faculty soon after I returned to Harvard from Oregon in 1986. The long-running ideological battle between the traditionalists and the smaller, but quite vocal CLS group was in full swing. Between 1986 and 1987, under circumstances that denied any claim of coincidence, the Harvard Law School denied tenure to four professors associated with Critical Legal Studies.[5] In the most noted case, the feminist-leftist legal scholar Clare Dalton was rejected when only a majority of the law faculty (and not the necessary two-thirds, supermajority) voted in favor of her appointment. Twelve members of a thirteen-person outside committee of scholars Harvard paid to examine Dalton's work found her work deserving of tenure.[6] Professor Laurence Tribe, a member of the liberal faction of Harvard's faculty complained: "If a young, relatively conservative male unconnected with Critical Legal Studies had written the same book [the manuscript submitted as a tenure piece by Dalton], I am morally confident that person would have been given tenure."[7] Harvard University President Derek Bok, asked by Law School faculty members to intervene, refused to overrule the vote—even though he had already vowed to strike down any tenure votes that appeared to be politically motivated.

Bok's vow proved one-sided. Within a few weeks of rejecting Dalton, David Trubek, a visitor at the Law School invited because of his leadership in an interdisciplinary area called "Law and Humanities," was voted tenure by the faculty. Like Dalton, Trubek was considered an adherent of Critical Legal Studies. This time, acting at the urging of faculty conservatives, Bok overruled the vote and rejected Trubek's appointment. It was the first time in the Law School's history that the university president had withdrawn a tenure offer approved by the faculty. In doing so, he called together a group of scholars, many of whom were thought to be hostile to Trubek's work, and claimed he relied on their recommendation.[8]

The liberal wing of the faculty was furious. I attended a dozen meetings of the Dalton-Trubek supporters. The faculty members who attended these informal sessions—virtually all tenured professors—were frustrated and upset. We were convinced that Dalton and Trubek had been treated unjustly and that their opponents had made a travesty of the tenure process. Even so, as typical academics, the group could never reach a consensus on any suggestions for serious and potentially successful action.

These professors focused on the possibility of writing a letter to protest the school's conduct and to attempt to convince Harvard to reverse itself. I saw this response as futile and tried to convince them that no written argument, no matter how intellectually fine-tuned, would cause the Law School to do what would amount to surrendering to us its power over appointments. Some of us did meet with President Bok, but he gave us no reason to hope he might reconsider his actions on either Dalton or Trubek. Finally, on June 1, 1987, I drafted a letter that expressed my feelings on the issue and my intention to mount a protest or, as I called it, "an academic vigil," which I invited the pro-Dalton and Trubek faculty members to join. During commencement week, I planned to remain in my office, taking meals, receiving visitors, and sleeping there. I explained: "I want to make a statement with my person, not merely with my words. Many will criticize my stand, but they cannot shake my conviction that all of us are responsible for the rejection of candidates who, by the standards applied here over many years, should have received the tenured appointments they sought and had earned."

Several faculty members praised my office sit-in and visited me during my vigil. None were willing to join me in it. Morton Horwitz brought me coffee, a doughnut, and the *New York Times* every morning at 7:30. Clare Dalton and her husband, Robert Reich, brought dessert to my office and shared it with me one evening. Jerry and Mary Jo Frug brought their two children and a beautiful dinner, including linen, china, and crystal. But while my office vigil created some media interest, and won personal commendations from students and the liberal public, my failure to gain the participation of other faculty members placed virtually no pressure on the administration. The Trubek and Dalton rejections were not reversed. To paraphrase the Scripture (James 2:26), intellect without action, like faith without works, standing alone, is dead.

Silent Acquiescence

Clare Dalton did file a sex discrimination complaint against Harvard University with the Massachusetts Commission Against Discrimination. Six years later, after a finding of "probable cause," and the institution of a suit charging Harvard with sex discrimination, both parties agreed in September 1992 to a settlement under which Harvard pledged to contribute $260,000 to a joint institute on domestic violence with Northeastern University where Dalton is now a tenured professor. Dalton suggested the settlement and will run the institute. Harvard will pay part of Dalton's legal expenses but denied any wrongdoing in the case.[9]

I will not contend that the diversity struggle at Harvard deserves greater priority than a program aimed at the horrors of domestic violence. And yet, the treatment of Dalton by the law faculty and the University that so enraged those of us who were her supporters would have made a very strong case, perhaps even one in which an appellate court might have ordered Harvard to actually start down the road toward true diversity which it maintains it is so willing to travel, but on which it has done so little for so long. For Harvard, a generous settlement offer combined with a denial of liability seems always the easier course. Relying on its prestige to shift the blame to those who protest its faults seems always the easier way.

Because the solo protester acts alone, usually without either seeking or obtaining approval from others who share his or her views, the protest is vulnerable to the charge that it was opportunistic and self-promoting, intended to advance some selfish, personal agenda rather than the ends of the protest movement. This is a common immediate reaction of those who do not share your views. Describing why many are reluctant to become whistle-blowers or to protest even heinous conditions, Taylor Branch says it has the undignified air of "loud shouting in a hushed museum, or of grandstanding. It is associated with scandal sheets, zealots, people who oversimplify the world into good and evil without room for the murky truth, who lack the quality of self-effacement in their enthusiasm for their own views."[10]

Some members of the Harvard faculty felt my protest was a pub-licity gimmick to sell my books. Erroneous media reports suggested that my protest would require that I give up my health coverage—a serious loss given my wife's illness. Professor Charles Fried lost his patrician bearing and accosted me across a crowded hallway. "You know damn well you won't lose your health coverage," he yelled. I acknowledged that he was correct and that the media report was in error. He was not much mollified. For him, the possibility that I had misled the press about my health coverage to enhance the sacrifice I was making was far more important than the salary loss I, in fact, would take.

Many more faculty members, apparently, were upset by what they perceived to be the actual goal of my protest, which they inferred from a comment I made when I announced my protest leave at the student rally. In urging that the Law School move promptly to hire and tenure a woman of color, I said: "And let there be no mistake. The goals of diversity will not be served by persons who look black and think white." The line drew applause from the students who wanted not just a woman of color but one who would bring a mi-nority viewpoint to her teaching and her interactions at the school.

Late that afternoon, Professor Randall Kennedy came to my office, quite visibly upset. Without our usual friendly banter, he came right to the point. "Several of our colleagues have come to my office to say they thought your comment about looking black and thinking white was unfair." "Interesting," I replied, "none of them have come to tell me directly." "Well," he sputtered, "they think you were talking about me. Were you?" Kennedy had upset much of the black community by a long *Harvard Law Review* article that was unfairly critical of a good deal of minority scholarship.[11] I had told him privately of my disagreement with that piece, but I answered quite honestly. "No, I did not have you in mind when I made my off-the-cuff statement." "Well," he responded, "when you made the statement, a number of students turned, saw me, and started laughing." Kennedy was learning the hard way that the way of the individual protester is difficult—whatever his or her position.

Ian Haney-Lopez, a student at the time, later wrote of my comment: "[a]ccusations of bigotry and intolerance erupted almost instantaneously."[12] One letter published in the student newspaper charged that my statement represented intolerance in its purest form and established an orthodoxy of thought that African Americans must embrace or be excommunicated. The theme was elaborated on in several published criticisms of my position. That there were no women of color and, save for five black men on a faculty of sixty-five, no minority faculty members, all the school's obvious failings were easily eclipsed by my dire and devilish plot to institute an orthodoxy of racist thought. Haney-Lopez stated clearly in his article what perhaps I did not in my speech, that "there are ways of thinking about the world which are highly correlated with community ties, and thus with race, and these must be considered in faculty hiring."[13]

My point was one that I have made before and since that speech, and one that minority scholars and teachers prove every day. Critical race theory, for instance, is a new approach to legal theory pioneered by minority scholars. Practitioners, often through the device of either true stories and personal anecdotes or fictional tales, discuss the many ways in which race and law affect each other. There is no unitary perspective, nor does every minority scholar write about race—just as not every white female professor writes about gender. But, as a whole, the perspectives we bring to our work are shaped by having lived our whole lives thinking about and experiencing issues of race—perspectives that, until now, have been ignored by the legal establishment. As Patricia Williams writes: "Voices lost in the chasm speak from the slow eloquent fact of the chasm."[14]

We bring the vision of a contracts professor who has read the slavery contract of her grandmother; a torts instructor who examines torts of racist slurs and deprivations. These issues did not find their way into law reviews or classrooms until the minority scholars who thought and cared about them deeply introduced them—just as most issues of particular concern to women, like sexual harassment, job discrimination, and rape, were neglected until women were accepted into the legal hierarchy and made male legal scholars take notice of these issues. The exclusion of these topics, you can be certain, was as much the product of the ignorance of those who did not confront them in their everyday lives, as a calculated decision that the subjects were unworthy and ultimately subversive. The new diversity of thought that many minority scholars bring to legal academia is not served by minority professors who represent white agendas. Those interests and perspectives are already well represented on law faculties.

Maybe reaction to my protest would have been warmer if I had made an effort to involve others in my protest or chosen an action—such as letter writing—in which more of my colleagues were willing to join. The faculty's reaction, can, I believe, be attributed, at least in part, to a feeling that I had embarrassed them by leaving *them* somehow stranded and alone on this issue. This is often the reaction of those who apparently share the protester's view. For them, there is a sense of betrayal that the protester has failed to obtain either approval or a consensus regarding his or her protest. We should have done something, they seem to say, but only after we gained the group's consensus. Those skilled in community relations do favor achieving agreement before going ahead with a particular tactic. In their view, consensus is as important as action or progress. I don't disagree, but I find it embarrassing as well as unproductive to exhort people who seem content to complain loudly to everyone in the world except those with the authority to change the unjust policy or practice.

Often, I admit, I don't try. I learned the futility of seeking support during my job in the Civil Rights Division of the Justice Department. There were a half dozen or so other young lawyers—all white—

working in the Division. We were all committed and often got together on weekends to discuss civil rights issues and the frustrations of our work. When I told them about the order I had received to give up my NAACP membership, all of them were quiet, including at least one lawyer who had previously boasted to me that he was the only white man in his town who belonged to the NAACP. When I decided not to surrender my membership, the other young lawyers urged me to stay, and then commiserated with my decision to leave. The white NAACP member was particularly quiet.

Often, the choice of going it alone is viewed by friends as a rejection of them and your group. Professor Leroy Clark worked with me back in the early 1960s at the NAACP Legal Defense Fund. Several years later, as I drove him back to his hotel following dinner at my home, Clark let me know in no uncertain terms how much he and other LDF staff members had resented my solo confrontations with the director, Jack Greenberg. We had been reminiscing about our days at the Fund and our differences with Greenberg. Clark told me that I would invariably go off on my own in protesting to Greenberg about one or another policy that we all felt was wrong. Clark's angry attack came as a shock. Obviously, he had been harboring these strong feelings for several years. I simply listened and said very little. For the life of me, I can't remember preventing others from challenging Greenberg or any of them complaining to me about my tactics. Given Clark's outburst, I wondered whether the staff might have been more angry with me for protesting than with Greenberg for the actions that made protest necessary.

It is not pleasant to consider that one's protest action can cause more consternation to those you consider to be on your side than it does to those you know are in your way. As Camus warned, we must often go forward "with weapons in our hands and a lump in our throats."[15] We must face the difficult dilemma of choosing between two evils: injuring others as the price of serving our cause, which Camus labels expediency, or "ineffectual purity." If we do nothing, we

CONFRONTING AUTHORITY

not only sacrifice the cause to which we are committed, but do so knowing that others will also be hurt by our failure to fight.[16] Perhaps the protester should take comfort in the fact that, whatever course one selects, one will have to live nagged by doubt about that choice.

Not that the choice is easy or even fair. Probably the most painful aspect of my Harvard protest was that Regina Austin, a woman I considered not only a good colleague, but also a close and valued friend, may have felt that my action had not only destroyed her chances for a permanent appointment, but also added more trauma to Austin's long and challenging year. On the day following my protest, a *New York Times* story carried interviews with several students in her classes.[17] Most of the comments were positive, but the story focused—complete with their photos—on two white males who claimed that she was a poor teacher. The story and the unwanted publicity hurt Austin deeply. While she found the courage to complete the school year, she did not speak to me for years after.

I was pleased that most black women teaching law publicly supported my protest.[18] There were some though—including some I had known for years and had encouraged and mentored—who reacted quite adversely to my protest. It was months before any of them spoke to me directly, but in the meantime I learned through others that they resented the fact that I had announced my unpaid leave without first getting Austin's approval or at least giving her notice of my plans. They did not thank me for risking my own position to call national attention to the plight of black female academics and criticized me for taking the public lead on the issue. As one of them put it, "None of us elected Bell as our leader and spokesperson."

As to my failing to share my protest plans with Regina Austin, the women may have been right. At the time, though, consulting her seemed both unnecessary and unfair. Unnecessary because Austin seemed far more militant and insightful about whites and racism than I was. I found her writings invigorating and admired her outspoken statements on issues of race and gender. As to fairness, it seemed at the time an unfair burden to enlist Austin in my fight with Harvard. I had not consulted her before mounting a campaign that helped secure her visit. How could I approach her and ask whether she approved my putting my job on the line to support the student campaign to get minority women on the faculty? The permission would have been difficult for me to seek and her response even harder to follow had she said, "Don't do it." After all, I had already decided to go ahead despite my wife's reservations.

After long years of public involvement, I failed to consider how daunting it can be for a basically private person to be thrust suddenly into a very controversial spotlight. I should have considered my own devastating experience a few years before during a one-semester visit at the Stanford Law School, where my teaching ability became a public issue. A month or so into the term, a delegation of outraged black students came to my office and reported that the Law School had responded to student complaints about my teaching not by approaching me, but by quietly setting up a series of lectures by other professors to insure that my students would gain from the lectures what it was feared they were missing in my course. To shield the real purpose of the lectures, I was invited to present one of them. It is hard to understand the magnitude of this insult without knowing the length to which schools will go to cover up the misconduct or incompetence of faculty members and to ignore students' frequently justified complaints. Yet Stanford neither defended me nor even consulted me about the complaints.

When the black students protested, the lectures were canceled. I accepted the school's apologies, but insisted on writing a long essay on the affair, copies of which I sent to every law school in the country with a request that the matter be discussed in faculty meetings.[19] It was not easy to concede that my teaching ability had been put in question, but I publicized the incident in the hope that other minority law teachers, subjected to similar experiences, would gain a better understanding of such student criticism. A few years later, I presented a lecture at Stanford and Dean Paul Brest offered me a public apology on behalf of the school. Significantly, at the time, Stanford students were engaged in a major effort to gain more minority representation on the faculty.

It is not difficult to find my failure to consider the effect of my protest on Regina Austin both selfish and sexist. Selfish in that the protester's voluntary sacrifice of privacy, security, and the warmth of group identity carries with it the risk of involuntary sacrifice of those interests by loved ones and friends. As to sexism, I had conceded in my speech at the student rally that there was a patriarchal element in my protective feelings about the black women students. I viewed these women as both my students, to whom my greatest obligation was to teach by example, and surrogates for the daughters I never had.

I have been spared the deep sense of inadequacy that must come to a father who, jobless, cannot provide bread for his family's table, but I have experienced the frustration of watching the thus far futile efforts of my daughters who look like me, and by extension those who are white but are no less my charges. I have watched them—and the men who stand with them—drafting the petitions, attending the rallies, standing in the vigils, sitting long nights in the dean's office, and experienced the pain of not being able to help them secure a most urgent component of their legal training. I determined to help these students come what may.

Some black women teachers, unaware of my motives, charged that my emphasis on their potential as role models for the black women students on whose particular behalf I protested had the effect of obscuring their skills and accomplishments.[20] Ironically, their argument was similar to that which Regina Austin had made in "Sapphire Bound!" in analyzing the Crystal Chambers case. As Austin pointed out, the desire to help minority girls in a counselling program by hiring Chambers as a role model backfired for Chambers and became grounds for firing her when she did not conform to their requirements. The law professors worried that to stress their value as role models also would hurt them by detracting from the achievements that entitled them to positions on the Harvard law faculty regardless of their potential value as mentors. That they had not been hired, and were unlikely ever to satisfy the faculty's shifting and elitist standards, did not deter them from advancing this argument.

In addition, some of the women felt that I had deprived them of their right to speak for themselves. They had not requested me to be their advocate or to advance any arguments on their behalf. Although none of them had come forward to do so, that was understandable. A protest on their own behalf would have seemed even more obviously self-serving than my own. Furthermore, many women of color were still early in their careers. They did not have the professional or financial standing to enable them to take this kind of action or to command attention in this or similar ways. In any event, none of them elected me to this role and, based on the criticism many women raised about my "Chronicle of the 27th Year Syndrome," in *And We Are Not Saved*, it was clear they would not have done so.[21]

Indeed, in one of those cruel tricks of fate that outdoes fiction because the truth is hardly believable, I may have inadvertently placed women of color in law teaching in a position like that of the unfortunate young black women in my "Chronicle," in which an ailment puts a randomly selected group of black women to sleep for a few months and permanently deprives them of their professional skills— all because they have not received bona fide offers of marriage from black men. I had hoped that this allegory, in which a tragedy occurs that only black men could prevent, would motivate black males to shake off our societally imposed powerlessness, with all its unhappy attributes, and move us to act more responsibly in relationships with black women. My critics pointed out that the much desired sense of power and responsibility for black men came at too high a price— the further subjugation of black women. Moreover, the frightening facts in the allegory serve to silence and incapacitate young black women, so that they are unable to participate in the healthier black man/black woman debate the "Chronicle" was intended to promote.

In real life, women of color are totally excluded from Harvard and many other law schools and therefore have no way of changing the exclusionary policies. By acting out of my own frustration and powerlessness to correct this condition, I proved my willingness to do battle, but in a fashion that—according to some faculty members—will retard the hiring of minority women for years to come. Even if they are wrong, the difficulties my critics saw in the "Chronicle" may come home to haunt women of color seeking law teaching jobs. In addition, my action may make it harder for these women to express their honest views on my protest. If they express their support, it will seem self-serving, yet any reservations they express will be used by unabashed opponents of affirmative action to place them in the camp with those black beneficiaries of affirmative action who now deem such policies "demeaning" and in conflict with the great American principle of merit. The parallels are not precise, but if some women argue that I have harmed the cause I claim to support, I can hardly dismiss their criticism as groundless.

If there is a moral or at least a lesson here, it is that individual protests are a disruptive anomaly. They interject into a conflict an element of uncertainty and the potential for chaos that is as likely to throw allies off stride as it is to cause opponents to reconsider their positions. Upset by the tension generated by the protest and, even more so, the debate that comes out of it, neither side wants to acknowledge that the protest has prompted a change—even a decisive change in the conflict.

Thus, just as Dean Albert Sacks assured me that my early 1970s letter advising him that I would not return the next year as the only black professor had nothing to do with the appointment of the second black faculty member, Clyde Ferguson, so Regina Austin and the black women law teachers who criticized my protest want deeply to believe that they are hired and promoted based on their ability. They view themselves as more than role models, as they should.

Silent Acquiescence

For reasons I had not expected, my efforts to exert the necessary pressure on behalf of Regina Austin and women of color generally received a level of public attention that caused them understandable unease. It was not that my protest made me their spokesperson. They quickly made the contrary quite clear. My protest, though, made it more difficult for them to believe what many blacks understandably want to believe: that we are selected and advanced based on our ability. We cling to that belief as fiercely—or even more fiercely—than the whites who claim to rely on it. We have struggled mightily to succeed, being measured and measuring ourselves by the standards that we are told are rational and, of course, objective. So when we finally arrive at whatever pinnacle we have sought, we wrap ourselves in the self-esteem now afforded by our positions and so long denied to us because of our race. Looked down on when at the bottom, we are not going to allow our accomplishments to be devalued when we've made it to (or near) the top.

The fact is, though, that most of us in law teaching—whatever our qualifications and potential—are the beneficiaries of pressures, past or present, on campus or beyond. That is why, as we should never forget, we hold tenured professorships at major, white law schools, when men like Charles Houston and William Hastie never did. If the presence of minorities in law teaching—albeit a nominal one—can be deemed progress, then we must recognize that progress exacted a price. The protester is one who, with all his or her faults, is willing to pay that price.

In his autobiography, *Lay Bare the Heart*, James Farmer, who founded The Congress of Racial Equality (CORE), recognized this fact. His most famous protest was his participation in the Freedom Rides, which he had helped organize but had not intended to join. But after saying goodbye to the CORE members, one young woman spoke with terror: "You're coming with us, aren't you, Jim?" After he gave several reasons why it would be unwise and simply impossible, she said: "Jim. Please." Without another word, Farmer got his luggage and boarded the bus.[22]

When jailed with other riders, Farmer received a letter from his wife, Lula. She recounted an exchange between the famous philosopher and civil disobedients Emerson and Thoreau: "Emerson, seeing Thoreau in jail, cried, 'Thoreau, my dear friend. What in the world are you doing in there?' Thoreau replied, 'Emerson, my dear friend. What in the world are you doing out there? This is the place for honest men in times like these.'"[23] Thoreau puts it well. One can hear the pride in his words, feel the joy in his heart. Thoreau was not boasting. He was recruiting, proselytizing really. Far from claiming victory, he was proclaiming the "Good News" about the self-affirming power of protest.

I believe that protest generates a magnetic force. Most of those within its field easily resist its attraction, but some respond with unexpected support. Again, James Farmer's experience is illustrative. Along with a group of friends in 1942, Farmer staged a sit-in in a restaurant in Chicago—where people claimed there was no Jim Crow segregation. Waitresses refused to serve them. Two whites who were not part of their group were served. One passed his food to the black man next to him, who began to eat. The other, a well-dressed middle-aged woman, just stared at her food. When asked by the waitress why she was not eating, she said, "It wouldn't be very polite for me to begin eating before my friends also have been served."[24] With that, some of the other customers stopped eating their meals. Desperate, the waitress called the police, who refused to expel the protesters. Finally, the Farmer group was served.

The support of a few whites in that restaurant made a great difference to the Farmer group's protest. It gave the sit-in legitimacy, presumably influencing both the police's decision not to arrest or interfere with the protesters and the restaurant management's decision to serve them. In addition, the effect on those who joined the protest must have been profound. Somehow, they saw an opportunity to involve themselves in a righteous cause, and they did it.

What moved these white people to defy the racial conventions of the time? The restaurant's Jim Crow policy, after all, was intended to affirm their superior status as whites. Was it that in the early 1940s America was waging a war against totalitarianism and bigotry? Was it that these protesters—black and white—were, at bottom, Americans too? Why, to bring the matter back home, did these strangers respond to Farmer's protest in a quiet but no less authenticating manner, while I was unable to gain solidarity from any of my white colleagues with whom I had worked for more than twenty years?

Is there not some point at which the sheer gut sense that something is wrong overpowers the pacifying effect of tenured status, the facile rationalizations of superior intellect? The answer is, in most instances, no. The white diners who supported James Farmer's sit-in deserve praise, but their support was anonymous and was unlikely to alter their status, threaten their jobs, or cost them their friends. Unless an individual is deeply moved or outraged on a profoundly personal level, there are simply too many constraints, too much experience that counsels caution rather than confrontation that is likely to incur enmity and to alienate one's associates. For most people, it is more prudent to work for change from within.

This was the choice Professor Laurence Tribe made. Perhaps the best known and certainly one of the most capable members of the Harvard Law faculty, Tribe had joined the faculty the same year I did. We had been friends over the years and generally found ourselves on the same side of faculty debates. He was a staunch supporter of recruiting more minorities and women for the faculty. Late in the second year of my protest when I returned to Cambridge to appeal the University's refusal to extend my leave, Tribe joined the meeting with Professors Frank Michelman and Charles Ogletree. He told us that he had become thoroughly disgusted with the Law School's hiring policies and had considered either joining my protest or simply resigning outright.

To put it mildly, I was excited! "Yes," I said to myself. "It can happen." Then Tribe added that, after discussing the matter, his family had convinced him that he could do more by remaining on the faculty and fighting from within. So, he explained, that is what he had decided to do.

My heart sank. Even as I agreed that his prestige would make his work from the inside far more effective than my own, I envisioned what his announcement of a protest leave or resignation would have meant to the diversity effort. The Law School and Harvard University could and did treat me as a troublesome but otherwise unimportant voice. They could not so cavalierly dismiss Tribe or, for that matter, any one of several white faculty members had they been willing to align themselves with my cause. I had commitment, but the whites had legitimacy. Institutions are far more likely to be influenced by prestige than passion.

Tribe has been true to his word. Publicly, he joined the faculty members who criticized the Law School in an open letter following the *Law Review*'s parody of Mary Jo Frug. Behind the scenes, I have no doubt that Tribe is continuing to work for a more diverse faculty. His efforts in this regard have been ineffective, but no more so than my own.

If Tribe had joined my protest, I think it would have made a difference. I cannot guarantee, though, that even his prestige would have moved the faculty to action so many believe is misguided and wrong. I could not, moreover, deny the risks involved in aligning himself with my protest. Important commissions or corporate clients might look elsewhere, a hoped for judicial appointment might not come, friends as well as enemies might question his motives, and he—like I—might inadvertently harm those he was trying to help. All of this and more are the penalties of protest. The failure to give these concerns serious consideration would be foolish. And, yet, I would have urged him to act.

In another context, someone has observed: "How fortunate are those who have never loved and lost. How fortunate and how sad." The message is clear. Pain and loss are the unavoidable risks for those

Silent Acquiescence

in the throes of romantic joy. Similarly, while those who have never been moved to take individual action against wrongs visited upon themselves or others need never experience the perils of protest, they miss as well the unique feeling of those who, moved to action, willingly exchange what the world gives and can take away for the enormous satisfaction of joining with the Thoreaus of the world who—even through the prison bars—are able to call out with a God-given certainty, "This is the place for honest men [and women] in times like these."

EIGHT

Retaliatory Responses

*T*amar was overjoyed to see Timur installed in the Citadel. She had met him years before, recognized him as a likely leader, and—for a time—saw in him something more. Tall and lithe, he had a handsome chiseled face and long, flowing hair. In addition, he seemed determined to help his people in their struggle against the Citadel's oppression. It was only natural that Tamar took it upon herself to introduce Timur to the Citadel. She made sure that he understood all of its unspoken rules and that he made no mistakes that would mar his performance as the first lowlander to enter the Citadel.

Their friendship blossomed, but Tamar was troubled. Did she resist romance because Timur, for all his talents and education, was a lowlander and not of her heritage? She hoped not. Still, increasingly, she and Timur seemed to be operating on different tracks, ones not necessarily parallel. Her concerns were, in time, destined to grow into fear and misgiving.

At first, Timur sat quietly during the Council meetings, absorbing everything he heard and saw. Of course, the Elders did not want him to assert himself. But if he did, he was but one voice and one vote, and they could safely ignore whatever he said. But then one day Timur did speak up, and the Elders were delighted to find that his views meshed almost exactly with their own. No one was more eloquent than Timur in urging that the harshest steps be taken to stamp out any further revolt among the lowlanders.

125

CONFRONTING AUTHORITY

Not privy to these secret meetings, the lowlanders could only watch the Citadel from the distance. They had claimed victory when Timur joined the Citadel. And now they waited to see how the representative for whom they had risked so much would relieve the misery of their lives. Over time, a few other lowlanders were admitted, but the Council found their accomplishments crude and unpolished in comparison with their own. Their intentions were good, but they had almost no influence with the Council. Timur had opposed them as unqualified and, in his effort to become a true Citadelian, treated them as badly as any of the Elders.

> I done what was right: white man takin everything
> Virgil Jones had, then goin to start on me—I weren't
> goin to let him do it without a fight. And had nothin
> ever shook me—when they shot me it didn't shake me,
> when they arrested me it didn't shake me. But it shook
> me to see my friends was but few.
>
> —Nate Shaw[1]

The human tendency to hope for a better day, rather than to work and run risks for it, is particularly strong when a confrontation with those in authority would endanger one's physical safety or economic well-being. It is not easy to predict what Frances Fox Piven and Richard Cloward refer to as "those always brief and usually unpredictable periods when large numbers of lower class people are roused to indignation and defiance."[2] The civil rights movement of the 1960s and the anti–Vietnam War demonstrations of the 1970s, not to mention the sudden downfall of seemingly invincible Communist nations in Eastern Europe and elsewhere, all are illustrations that mass uprisings can happen. When they do, individual participants in those movements perform heroic acts, often at tremendous personal cost.[3]

Occasionally, as with Mrs. Rosa Parks's refusal to move from the

Retaliatory Responses

white section of a Montgomery bus, an individual protest can spark a major movement. But this is far more often the exception than the rule. Indeed, Mrs. Parks's action was, if not planned, a timely catalyst for blacks who had been organizing for some time to mount an antisegregation campaign.[4] In the all too typical case, though, the Rosa Parkses of the world will mount their protests on their own only to become even more alone, criticized more often than praised. The silence and sometimes the active opposition of one's friends is the most painful part of any protest action. Solo protests strain or may even sever highly valued relationships which are seldom ever repaired. Whatever his or her courage in challenging powerful authority, the protester is not invincible. Virtually all are vulnerable to, and some are unable to survive, attacks from within their ranks. None of my protests involved the risks or resulted in the losses suffered by the protesters discussed in this chapter. The patterns of response from both opponents and supporters, though, are quite similar and provide important lessons in what the repercussions of confronting authority can be.

No one, particularly a black person, should launch a serious protest alone without full awareness of what happened to the great singer and actor Paul Robeson. Also a Rhodes Scholar and Columbia Law School graduate, Robeson devoted the last half of his life, in the pre–civil rights movement days of the 1950s and early 1960s, to campaigning against the often violent manifestations of racism in this country. Taking on any and every injustice, Robeson worked to end lynchings, the Korean War, Jim Crow laws, colonialism in Africa, and discrimination in immigration, in labor laws, and even in baseball, among other things. In his career as a singer and actor, he took a strong stand against segregation, refusing to perform in the South or anywhere audiences were segregated.

Obviously, Robeson felt the dilemma of the outsider granted conditional permission to come inside. Martin Duberman's detailed biography of him summarizes Robeson's resolve to take a stand on issues of racial and social justice:

He moved from the view that his own accomplishments would open doors for others to the conviction that the doors remained so firmly secured that those who had somehow pushed through them had to see to their permanent dismantling as a primary obligation. During the years of Roosevelt's New Deal, Robeson remained reasonably hopeful that white America would itself recognize the worst aspects of institutionalized racism and work to expunge them. . . . He never ceased being an American patriot—continuing to believe in the inspirational promise of the country's principles, if not her practice—but the more white America failed, in the post–World War II years, to stand up for the rights of people of color, the more Robeson grew into a militant spokesman for the world's oppressed. The country's failure to set its house in order, to ransom its own promise, brought out in him not—as in so many others—weary acquiescence but, rather, uncompromising anger, a dogged refusal to bow.[5]

Ignoring his agent's warning that he was doing himself "a great deal of harm," Robeson risked everything and lost everything.[6] Refusing to temper his critique at a time when America's witch hunt for communists, not coincidentally, tarred many of the country's most vocal critics, Robeson was labeled a Party member and made an outcast. Towns where he was scheduled to sing canceled his performances, sparking a pattern that was to follow him across the country. At times, Robeson was given permission to sing as long as he did not talk to an audience; but, refusing to give in, he sang songs with pointedly political lyrics.[7] Radio and television stations, recording studios, and theatre and film companies barred Robeson entirely.[8] His salary dropped from over $100,000 to less than $6,000 per year.[9] A total pariah, Robeson was denounced in Congress, burned in effigy, and threatened with violence. The government had the F.B.I. follow him and intercept his mail and phone conversations, and he was denied the right to leave the country unless he agreed not to make speeches.[10] Robeson would not agree.

Not surprised when whites turned away from him, Robeson dismissed their criticism with a confidence few blacks dared—then, or now. He wrote in his autobiography, *Here I Stand*:

> At the outset, let me make one thing very clear, I care nothing—less than nothing—about what the lords of the land, the Big White Folks, think of me and my ideas. For more than ten years they have persecuted me in every way they could—by slander and mob violence, by denying me the right to practice my profession as an artist, by withholding my right to travel abroad. To these, the real Un-Americans, I merely say: "All right—I don't like *you* either!"[11]

Robeson, though, was shocked and stunned by the open hostility of the black establishment. Jackie Robinson, who had benefitted from Robeson's work against discrimination in professional baseball, testified against Robeson before the House Committee on Un-American Activities.[12] The baseball player's prepared statement was carefully worded only to condemn as "silly" Robeson's assertion that blacks would not fight for this country. He defended Robeson's right to his personal views and acknowledged the real injustices blacks suffer.[13] Robeson's enemies really didn't care what Jackie Robinson said. That he appeared before the Committee was comment enough—especially to the press, which eagerly reported the criticism in Robinson's remarks, while ignoring their general tenor. In their turn, the leaders of the major civil rights organizations deemed it important to prove their own loyalties by condemning Robeson.[14]

Virtually alone, and his career over, Robeson still refused the government's invitation to deny that he was a member of the Communist Party. When reporters asked him if he was not hurting his cause by allying with communists, Robeson angrily responded: "Is that what you want? For me to bend and bow and shuffle along and be a nice, kindly colored man and say please when I ask for better treatment for my people?—Well, it doesn't work."[15]

CONFRONTING AUTHORITY

Like a sadly small number of others, he stood on his Fifth Amendment rights before HCUAA. In a hearing before the Committee in 1956, Robeson reiterated his commitment to defending his rights, whatever the personal cost. When a senator derisively asked him why he did not live in the Soviet Union, Robeson responded: "Because my father was a slave, and my people died to build this country, and I am going to stay here and have a part of it just like you."[16]

The last years of Robeson's life were dominated by physical and mental illness. Severe depression, which caused him to try to take his life, confined him to mental institutions and then to his home. While unable to determine a cause of his illness, his doctors were never able to discount the contribution of the years of public hostility and hounding to his poor health.

Confronted with the enormous and unrewarded pain a lone protester like Paul Robeson suffered as a result of his courageous advocacy, there is the obvious question: was the cause worth the suffering and sacrifice? Because Robeson stood alone, it was all too easy for an already hostile country to isolate him and dismiss him as either a puppet or a lunatic. But individual protests create a magnetic field of their own with a power and influence beyond anything that happens to the protester. As was the case with Dick Gregory's seemingly ignored Olympic protest, Robeson obviously reached some people. A black prisoner at Marion State Penitentiary in Illinois wrote of Robeson after his death:

> They knocked the leaves
>   From his limbs
> The bark
>   From his
>   Tree
> But his roots
>   were
>   so deep
> That they are a part of me.[17]

Regrettably, Robeson likely heard too little of how much he was revered by working-class blacks, those who respect action more than position, defiant deeds more than fancy rhetoric. W. E. B. Du Bois's experience was almost identical to Robeson's.[18] He was harassed by the government, tried and acquitted in 1951 when he was eighty-three years old on the charge of acting as a foreign agent, and had his passport withdrawn. In his own field, he could not find publishers for his writing or colleges at which to lecture. Also like Robeson, he was abandoned, or, worse, condemned by the mainstream black leadership.[19] The NAACP fired him and later warned its branches to have nothing to do with him. In both Robeson's and Du Bois's cases, though, their early fame resulted in a too tardy but no less appreciative recognition of their courageous stand. Years later, Jackie Robinson, wiser and himself disillusioned by the lack of civil rights progress, expressed regret for having condemned Robeson: "I would," he wrote, "reject such an invitation if offered now. . . . I have grown wiser and closer to painful truths about America's destructiveness."[20]

Robinson's willingness to admit his error is characteristic of a man who fought as hard for black progress off the playing field as he did in breaking the color barrier in baseball. Muhammad Ali, though, was perhaps the most courageous protester of all professional athletes, regardless of race. While his clowning and rhyming likely endeared him to whites as much as his boxing skills, he was always serious about racial discrimination. Having won a gold medal in the 1960 Olympics in Rome, Ali returned home to Kentucky where he found: "With my gold medal actually hanging around my neck, I couldn't get a cheeseburger served to me in a downtown Louisville restaurant."[21] To make a statement on the country's hypocrisy on racial matters, Ali threw the medal into the Ohio River.

This country now expects blacks to protest blatant racial discrimination; as Dr. King and Dr. Du Bois learned, though, there is no tolerance for blacks who actively protest America's war policies. A member of the Nation of Islam, Ali refused to serve in Vietnam on religious grounds, declaring, "I'm not going ten thousand miles from

CONFRONTING AUTHORITY

here to help murder and kill and burn poor people simply to help continue the domination of white slave masters over the darker people."[22]

Ali reported to the induction center in Houston, as ordered. His name was called three times, and each time Ali stayed in his place and refused to be inducted. He told the story this way:

> That day in Houston in '67 when I went to the induction center, I felt happy, because people didn't think I had the nerve or they don't have the nerve to buck the draft board of the government. And I almost ran there, hurried. I couldn't wait to not take the step. And then when I did that, all the boys looked surprised. The guy that asked me to take the step looked surprised, and we went into the back room and they talked to me, told me what's going to happen. If I go, I don't have to fight, or just do exhibitions and things. I told them I still won't go, because that's leading more boys to death. And I says, I'd rather go to jail. So they say, "You're going to get there," and I never did.
>
> How I felt going there? The world was watching, the blacks mainly, looking to see if I had the nerve to buck Uncle Sam, and I just couldn't wait for the man to call my name, so I wouldn't step forward. I enjoyed that day.[23]

Ali was indicted, tried, and sentenced to five years imprisonment. Although he was freed on bail pending appeal, he was stripped of his boxing championship title and was not allowed to fight. Interestingly, while several prominent African American leaders backed Ali, civil rights leaders were silent. Three years later, after once rejecting his appeal and after deadlocking on the issue of his religious convictions, the Supreme Court overturned Ali's conviction on the ground that the F.B.I. had illegally wiretapped his telephone.[24]

Nate Shaw[25] and Hosea Hudson,[26] other black men who saw communism as the answer to American racism, fared less well. There were, as well, those men and women whose commitment to the civil rights cause brought them more misery than success, more ridicule than rec-ognition.[27] Whatever their target, most individual protesters will stand alone.[28] It comes as no surprise that those in authority who are the protest's objects usually resent the message and almost always set out to punish the messenger. The complainant or his or her tactics are attacked in an effort to deflect attention from the substantive issue. Paul Robeson's enemies made an issue of his loyalty and political as-sociation rather than the racial injustice about which he was protest-ing. For different reasons, and with even greater effect, those who should be or claim to be sympathetic to the protester or his or her cause (like the black establishment that showed Paul Robeson no mercy) will join in the attack.

The hostile response of friends and associates is complex, unex-pected, and far more devastating than enemies' predictable attacks. Black leaders surely knew that Robeson's attacks on American racism were accurate. They decided, though, that he had "gone too far," and feared that by connecting the disease of American racism with the cure of communism, he was endangering all black people. For this reason, as one major black lawyer once told me, they had to "cut him off."

To a lesser degree, black leaders also distanced themselves from Martin Luther King's statements about the Vietnam War and the need to address economic injustice. After King gave his first major speech against U.S. policy in Vietnam, both Roy Wilkins and Bayard Rustin, two prominent black leaders, disassociated themselves from him. Even King's closest advisers disagreed with his decision to take a stand against the war, worrying that it would undermine his cred-ibility and alienate the president and important supporters of the civil rights movement.[29] The NAACP's Board of Directors issued a state-ment that described the attempt to merge the civil rights and peace movements as "a serious tactical mistake"—a move that the *New York Times* reported under the front-page headline, "NAACP Decries Stand of Dr. King on Vietnam."[30]

Carl Rowan, the black journalist, criticized King's antiwar stance in a widely circulated *Reader's Digest* piece, writing that King's "tragic decision" to speak against the Vietnam War "has alienated many of the Negro's friends and armed the Negro's foes."[31] In an editorial, the *Washington Post* summarized the view of King's critics. King, the staff wrote, "has done a grave injury to those who are his natural allies . . . and . . . an even graver injury to himself. Many who have listened to him with respect will never again accord him the same confidence. He has diminished his usefulness to his cause, to his country, and to his people. And that is a great tragedy."[32]

Evidently, out of concern that they will be lumped in the same unpopular heap, moderate supporters will punish the protester whose speech or action—even when taken in their behalf—they deem too radical. Others, while claiming allegiance to the cause, will disparage the protester's actions or motives in order to justify—both to themselves and those around them—their own inaction. Perhaps the hardest criticism to take is that leveled by those like Ralph Bunche, the black United Nations Under-Secretary, who chastised Dr. King publicly for his stand, and then called him to express his private agreement.[33]

King answered his critics with his commitment. King was neither surprised nor ultimately shaken by the hostility to his outspoken opposition to the Vietnam War. Knowing the reaction he could expect, King had vacillated for a long period of time before denouncing the war. Ultimately, he decided to speak up, and later explained that he could not be silent about an "issue that is destroying the soul of our nation." To King, speaking out against the war in Vietnam, like his civil rights fight, was simply another cross he must bear: "The cross may mean the death of your popularity. It may mean the death of a foundation grant. It may cut down your budget a little, but you take up your cross, and just bear it. And that's the way I have decided to go."[34]

Retaliatory Responses

King, of course, experienced opposition from nominal allies long before he raised his sights beyond racial issues. In his famous Letter from a Birmingham Jail, King responded to critical clergy members who charged that his marches were disruptive and ill-timed. The clergy's published statement called the nonviolent direct-action crusade "unwise and untimely." They described King as an "outside agitator" who was not giving Birmingham's new, more moderate (but still segregationist) leadership a chance. Dr. King answered his critics point by point. He responded to their criticism by expressing his own disappointment with the white church and its leadership. He mentioned individual church leaders who were exceptions, but reported that many ministers, priests, and rabbis had been "outright opponents, refusing to understand the freedom movement and misrepresenting its leaders. All too many others," he added, "were more cautious than courageous and remained silent behind the anesthetizing security of stained-glass windows." King then observed:

> In the midst of blatant injustices inflicted upon the Negro, I have watched white churchmen stand on the sideline and mouth pious irrelevancies and sanctimonious trivialities. In the midst of a mighty struggle to rid our nation of racial and economic injustice, I have heard many ministers say: "Those are social issues, with which the gospel has no real concern." And I have watched many churches commit themselves to a completely otherworldly religion which makes a strange, un-Biblical distinction between body and soul, between the sacred and the secular.[35]

The solo protester must expect criticism from those, like the clerics, who consider themselves allies but do not feel the same urgency and willingness to sacrifice. While emphasizing their agreement with your goals, they will sigh with relief as they find some reason to disagree with your means; they will point to the protester's method, timing, delivery, or perceived "grandstanding" as convenient justification for their own inaction.

The impulse to obey authority and the reluctance to confront it are deeply ingrained in the human psyche. In the wake of the Nuremberg trials, in an effort to understand why people obeyed the inhuman commands of Nazi leaders, a number of theorists began studying the dynamics of this type of social submission. In what is probably the best known of these studies, *Obedience to Authority*, Stanley Milgram reports his findings.[36] Milgram asked participants in his experiments, under a variety of circumstances, to administer what they believed to be electric shocks as the subject screamed and begged for mercy. Although many of the testees later said that they had been repelled by the order to administer the shocks, a significant majority did so anyway. Shocked by his own findings, Milgram tried to discover what it is in human nature or social organization that makes people unwilling to resist authority figures, even when they hurt others and betray their own consciences in the process. Milgram identified several reasons, including the tendency to deny responsibility for one's actions when "only following orders"; the need to belong and be accepted; and the social mores that prevail at home, at school, and at work, which punish dissent and nonconformity. Most people's unwillingness to defy authority, or support others who do—even when the orders are bad, even evil—is the unhappy side effect of the willingness to follow leadership, which is apparently basic to any social order.

Milgram's findings parallel the experience of Daniel Ellsberg, the former government official who leaked what became known as the Pentagon Papers, a voluminous set of classified documents that provided evidence that the government had lied to the public about its conduct in the Vietnam War. During a year of intense soul searching before he released the material to newspapers, Ellsberg found few people who believed that his proposed course of action was either prudent or likely to be effectual. While Ellsberg expected to be condemned by government insiders and to be jailed, he seemed surprised by the hostility his actions met with from colleagues at the RAND Corporation, including some close friends.[37] Referring to a letter to the *New York Times* which he and other RAND employees signed and in which they called for unilateral withdrawal from Vietnam, Ellsberg recalls: "What the reactions to the letter within RAND revealed very strikingly was a pervasive fear . . . that their jobs would be immediately threatened along with their whole way of life, which on the whole was a quite good one." Even concern that his public position would diminish the institution's credibility and influence were secondary to the fear that "they would lose their jobs merely by virtue of the fact that a colleague—a few handfuls of colleagues—registered agreement with the position . . . held by a majority of the American public."[38]

A few of his co-workers told Ellsberg that they would have signed the letter except they had to think of their alimony payments or children's tuition. Their rationalizations, Ellsberg said, seemed "greatly to magnify the inevitable material losses that would accompany doing something that one has decided for whatever closely calculated reasons not to do."[39] He continued:

> [W]hen people are questioning their own reasons for not spilling something, they really have to come up with satisfactory reasons to continue to withhold some information or to refrain from taking some decisive action. And those reasons cannot be that they're cowardly or not very patriotic or inhumane or excessively concerned about their careers. Those are just not satisfying over a period of time.

To release themselves from the dictates of their consciences, these people magnify the risks associated with the action they contemplate. In their minds, the likely sacrifice becomes so big and the potential payoff so minor that they can conclude with assurance that no rational person would forge ahead in such circumstances. Why feel guilty for not venturing where only fanatics do not fear to tread?

In an insidious manipulation of priorities, the disruption caused by the protesters' efforts are viewed as a greater evil than the injustice that the protesters act against. Thus, King's suffering in being jailed in Birmingham is subordinated to the suffering of the white ministers who argued that he had imperiled the orderly, gradual operations needed to resolve the city's crisis. They blamed King, and not those who regularly discriminated against blacks, for the current disturbance. Dr. King, like most protesters, became a two-time victim: of the misconduct he protested and of the misdirected anger of those around him.

No protest, of course, will ever be without flaws. I have yet to discover any action so precise in its means and so elegant in its delivery that its unmitigated success is assured. To the contrary, most single-handed protests—and many movements—will not accomplish their goals. What separates the protester from those who stand aside and debate and critique—seemingly without end—is the protester's sense of personal urgency and the recognition that, in the real world, we cannot expect—and certainly should not wait for—the perfect solution. He or she will risk failure in the hope of finding that intangible relief and self-fulfillment that comes from the protest itself.

Unlike those who chastised King, most allies-cum-critics nurse their disapproval silently, although nonetheless obviously. Some will even echo your outrage and pledge their help but somehow never turn up when needed. The whispered criticism of those you consider friends and the often made but never delivered upon promises are the most hurtful responses to the person who challenges authority. As Dr. King recognized when he wrote from a Birmingham jail, still chastising the white ministers who claimed to be his allies: "Shallow understanding from people of good will is more frustrating than absolute misunderstanding from people of ill will."[40] Mute criticism undermines even more effectively because it allows no debate. The protester loses the energizing possibility of responding to the concerns, persuading the critic, even occasionally unmasking those whose objections often have little to do with the propriety of the protest itself.

Retaliatory Responses

My friend Lawrence Watson, a former assistant dean at the Harvard School of Design, learned firsthand the protester's vulnerability to the deceit of his opponents and the silence of his friends. In the 1987–88 school year following my return to Harvard from Oregon, Watson and I agreed to serve as co-chairs of the Black Faculty and Administrators of Harvard University. The group decided to look into the University's minority hiring record for faculty and staff, which was far worse than the Law School's and a source of our continuing concern. In a meeting with then president Derek Bok, we offered to meet individually with the academic deans to get their views on the minuscule number of minority faculty and staff members in their schools. Bok gave the project his blessing. Several of us met with each dean, prepared summaries of our conversations, and submitted them to the deans for revisions and corrections.

The challenge then, as with all civil rights reports, was to prepare and issue a report that would not simply be read, filed, and forgotten. I spent much of the summer writing a summary of Harvard's affirmative action performance that could not be so easily ignored. The report, mostly in fictional form, reviewed the data we had obtained and suggested that if all of Harvard's black faculty and staff, along with Harvard's president, were killed in an unexplained explosion, the tragedy would inspire all in the community to move aggressively to hire blacks and other minorities. I suggested that such an action would be no less appropriate without a tragic motivation. Members of our group were not enthusiastic about the report's form, and Watson worked hard to overcome their resistance, particularly the argument that was repeatedly made to him privately, "Bell is tenured, but most of us staff people can be dismissed at the end of the year." Watson persevered and obtained sufficient support to publish the report. President Bok was not amused by my effort to use a parable to illustrate the point that civil rights reform at Harvard, as elsewhere, would require a crisis as a catalyst. Little discernible action that was positive resulted from this protest and, as many in our group had warned,

CONFRONTING AUTHORITY

Larry Watson lost his job—ostensibly for budget reasons—at the end of the school year. I represented Watson at an administrative hearing, held under University rules, and built a record strongly indicating that disagreement with his civil rights activities, more than budget concerns, prompted the dean to fire him. While not admitting wrongdoing, the University settled the case. During the lengthy administrative proceeding, the black faculty and staff provided no support and maintained a rather distant silence.

On another campus, Professor Karen Fields, in May 1992, expressed the pain and loneliness of this unexpected silence. In an open letter to her colleagues, she announced her resignation as director of black studies at the University of Rochester.[41] In addition to a range of opposition to her affirmative action efforts, she had taken a public position against the discrimination she and her husband, a talented civil engineer, experienced in the labor market. Only five faculty members accompanied her to a meeting with local officials to which she had invited her colleagues.

> And despite the fact that this protest was reported in the newspaper and on television, that episode and the problems it pointed to were met with resounding silence—silence from well-positioned Rochester old-timers, silence on campus, silence from well-wishers in the city, silence from those who never stop incanting that desegregation would be achieved in many domains, if only qualified minority candidates could be found, silence from those who stand daily before mixed classes and implicitly say that skills gained through hard work will open doors, silence from those whose outrage would be loud—in fact, both loud and listened to—if they thought a black person was being given something he had not earned—in short, stunning and nearly universal silence, broken only by a tiny handful of colleagues.

It is not necessary to review whether those who disappointed Professor Fields were justified in their absence. Her letter, though, speaks eloquently for all of us who have needed support that is expected—even promised—and then withheld. Indeed, the silence of many who you suppose are on your side is so predictable that protesters must consider it part of the risk of confronting authority.

As in my friend Larry Watson's case, the major reason for silence or nonaction is concern that the authority will use its power to make life difficult for those who assist the troublemaker. These are usually well-founded fears. "Whistle-blowers"—the rather derisive term describing individuals within an organization who challenge authority by reporting unlawful, corrupt, or unsafe conditions in government or corporations—often find themselves in uncomfortable and often dangerous positions.[42] Such risks the New York City police officer Frank Serpico accepted when he broke ranks to reveal the pervasive corruption in the department. The terrifying story of Karen Silkwood, a technician and union activist at the Kerr-McGee nuclear power plant in Oklahoma, provides another example of what can happen to someone whose conduct threatens to undermine those in power.[43] Silkwood's disclosure of the plant's lax safety procedures created a national, industrywide scandal. Contaminated by nuclear radiation at the plant, Silkwood testified before the Atomic Energy Commission about serious procedural violations at the plant. She agreed to collect evidence that company officials had tampered with records in order to disguise the practices which violated the law and endangered workers. On her way to meet a *New York Times* reporter with documents she had gathered, Silkwood was killed in a suspicious car accident. That evidence disappeared. And despite their important contributions, both Silkwood and Serpico were ostracized by their peers and distrusted by many outsiders.

Despite the protection of federal and state laws, companies utilize, often with the acquiescence of other employees, a chilling array of tactics to harass, intimidate, and punish whistle-blowers. As Glazer and Glazer describe, the tactics include "attacking the source's motives, professional competence, economic credibility, sexuality, or virtually anything else that will work to cloud the issue" (224). Whistleblowers may be transferred to a "bureaucratic Siberia," or assigned to clean up the mess, then denied the authority and staff to do the job and subsequently fired for their failure to perform. Whistle-blowers may be laid off even as the company is hiring new staff. The counter-moves are designed both to neutralize the complainants and convey the message to other personnel that troublemakers will suffer serious consequences.[44]

Serpico's and Silkwood's stories were both told in feature films (in 1978 and 1983, respectively), films that are significant only in that they demonstrate popular interest in, if not popular support for, whistle-blowers. Regrettably, there is no feature film about Fannie Lou Hamer, an uneducated black sharecropper from a town called Ruleville, Mississippi.[45] Fannie Lou Hamer became active in the voting rights movement in 1962, when a team of civil rights workers arrived in town, trying with little success to get the black residents to register to vote. Mrs. Hamer was among the first to make the trip to the courthouse. When she returned, having been told she failed the literacy section of the exam (none of the group was passed), she was kicked off the farm on which she worked with her husband. From that day on, as Hamer traveled the South to encourage others to register, the Hamers were harassed by private citizens and local authorities alike. Once, Mrs. Hamer received a $9,000 water bill, which she protested. How, she asked, could she owe so much when her house had no running water?[46]

Kay Mills, in her comprehensive biography of Fannie Lou Hamer, describes what this remarkable woman was put through for her work to register, feed, and educate blacks in Mississippi:

> Not only had she lost her job and been jailed and beaten for her voter-registration efforts, she had telephone threats against her life and had heard that a black man had been hired to kill her. . . . One of the SNCC workers said she would be campaigning in the "roughest territory in the world outside of South Africa." It was fantastic, he said, "to be planning a campaign where a pri-

mary consideration is whether the candidate will get killed." Later she would receive hate mail—including a heart with a dagger through it—from out of state after her testimony at the 1964 Democratic National Convention. She had a matter-of-fact response to the threats, saying that she was never sure when she left home whether she'd get back. "Sometimes it seems like to tell the truth today is to run the risk of being killed. But if I fall, I'll fall five-feet four-inches forward in the fight for freedom."[47]

The reprisals that a lone protester suffers play, and are intended to play, to a much wider audience. The sanctions are meant not only for the particular protesters taking action, but also for those who would dare to follow them. Whatever form the expected retribution may take—loss of a job or the possibility of promotion, violence or the too credible threat of violence—it is enough to keep many self-proclaimed sympathizers on the sidelines. Perhaps most demoralizing is the well-founded fear that challenging authority will leave one isolated and alone, either politically or, more fundamentally, personally. It is only human to want to belong, to be a part of the group, "one of the gang." Because the solo protester risks both personal security and group identity, he or she also faces estrangement from those who envy or resent the willingness to take risks they will not take. This resentment can manifest itself in a number of ways, none of them pleasant for the protester. Longtime friends simply drop out of sight or, when you do see them, make no mention of your protest. Sometimes, they join your opponents' criticism of your action, although they argue it is only for your own good or the good of your common cause.

Fannie Lou Hamer's fate is a sad and shameful illustration of what can happen to the lone protester. She was hospitalized twice for nervous breakdowns towards the end of her life. Later, when failing health forced her out of the movement, she was left alone, without financial or emotional support from those she had helped in her life. Kay Mills tells a heart-wrenching story of how Mrs. Hamer cried because she could no longer use her arms to comb her hair and no one would come to help her. Her husband complained:

> My wife loved people, but people didn't love her . . . I would come to this house and it would be so many people in here I couldn't hardly get in the door. They came to get clothes, food, money—everything. But when she fell sick and was in the hospital at Mount Bayou, the only way I could get people to stay with her was when I paid them. . . . She raised lots of money and she would come back and give it to people. And when she died, she didn't have a dime.[48]

When Dr. King extended his campaign against racial discrimination to encompass the war in Vietnam and unequal economic opportunity at home, he lost the support of many in the civil rights movement who agreed with King on both issues, but feared that taking on these issues would alienate many of those who had supported the civil rights movement on less controversial grounds. As with Paul Robeson, neither fame nor fortune insulates the protester deemed to have gone too far. Even Dr. W. E. B. Du Bois, probably the most brilliant intellectual in black history, was written off by most black leaders when he embraced socialism.

Time, of course, has vindicated the men and women who dared stand and protest loudly rather than quietly conform. Even as we hail their courage, a small doubt lingers. Can our tardy vindication today justify the agony they experienced then? Is the abuse they suffered an invitation to us, or is it a warning to give a comforting reading to the Beatitude, "The meek shall inherit the earth"? Surely, conformity, even with its burden of quiet guilt, is preferable to traumatic confrontations with powers whose lack of tolerance for criticism we can foresee as readily as we can expect, in the wake of our action, the silence of our friends.

NINE

Risks, Rewards, and Reaffirmation

The lowlanders began to question the Elders' good faith. With much respect, they petitioned the Citadel rulers to admit more of them to its ranks, or from the ranks of other disadvantaged peoples who had joined their struggles over the years. A goodly number of these residents had, in the intervening years, gone to school and worked, gaining experiences that would equip them to serve in the Council of Elders.

Few of the Citadel's rulers were moved by these requests. Besides, lulled by the relative peacefulness following Timur's admission, and the civility of the lowlanders' new demands, the Elders felt confident that they need make no further concessions. Even so, having learned a lesson, when the lowlanders requested a meeting, the Council did not wait this time for the lowlanders to rush the gates, but invited their representatives to a meeting to discuss their concerns. The lowlanders spoke first, their arguments carefully drafted in the language used by the members of the Citadel. Appealing to both law and justice, they argued that proportional representation of fifty percent lowlanders would benefit both groups.

The Council responded diplomatically, giving the answer Xercis had foreseen during their last encounter with the lowlanders. Xercis calmed their visitors by claiming to share their concerns. He regretted, he said, that a most serious and wide-ranging search had turned up no other lowlanders who merited entry. Pointing to the lowlander members, he reminded the lowlander outsiders that the Citadel had

145

demonstrated its commitment to reform. "It would be wrong," Xercis concluded, "to measure our reform by numerical gauges rather than the sincerity by which we have come so far in our mutual quest for reform." Some of the lowlanders—particularly those already inside— were reassured by—or, like Timur, agreed with him. Others among them recalled their history and their lives of subordination. They wondered if they hadn't made a terrible mistake in striking a deal with Xercis.

In the years that followed, the Citadel continued to add lowlander members to its ranks—always one at a time—and usually after one of the older lowlanders died, retired, or moved elsewhere. Each of them resembled Timur more than any of the less privileged lowlanders who had participated in the Great Revolt. Every so often, a delegation would come from the valley to question the slow pace of progress, and each time it would be greeted civilly by the Citadel's leaders. The discussion always proceeded on much the same terms. Then the delegation would depart, some of its members angry and some reassured—but nothing would have changed.

Tamar also watched and waited for change. She, too, had been confident that Timur's entry into the Citadel, and the admission of colleagues very much like him, would change the Citadel. But she finally had to recognize her mistake in thinking that the Citadel and her father would share their power so easily.

Tamar finally confronted Timur. "Have you forgotten that you were brought here to satisfy the aspirations of your people, and to represent them here in the halls of power?"

Timur did not try to conceal his arrogance and disdain. "I am here because I won the competition, and I deserved to win it. I owe nothing to you or to anyone else. As an Elder, I have heard the lowlanders' delegation and its pleas for justice. I must tell you that I find them misguided, ill-advised, and hopeless. No one here—myself included— will ever support their petitions. The lowlanders do not need justice. They do not need handouts. What they need is more discipline. With hard work and dedication, they can achieve what I have in my own life."

Risks, Rewards, and Reaffirmation

Tamar simply stared at this man—this stranger, her enemy. This man who, but for the color of his skin, was indistinguishable from any of the Elders—in his manner, his thoughts, and in his very being. And it was she who had brought him into the Citadel. Timur was her responsibility.

The fear in Timur's eyes when she pulled the long knife from her jacket was sweet revenge. She maneuvered him against the wall and raised the knife to his throat. Her voice was colder than the stone he cringed against. "What I threaten today your people will accomplish when they find you out. And, Timur, they will find you out." Then Tamar called for the guards. "Take me away," she said, calm now. "I have tried to kill a member of the Council of Elders."

Two decades ago, or more, the *New Yorker* magazine published a short story about a group of black trash collectors and their unbearably arrogant white supervisor. In the story, Jake, one of the black workers, is always trying to give his boss good advice about how to run his business. The supervisor resents the unsolicited suggestions and finally dismisses Jake. The other black workers shake their heads. "Well, we knew it would happen. Ole Jake done gone and got his damn self fired trying to teach the white folks."

Jake's assertiveness/subservience dilemma will strike a familiar chord for many Americans regardless of race, including some holding positions far loftier than manual laborer. If Jake had clowned around with his co-workers and followed his boss's orders to the letter—even when they were stupid—he would have kept his job, though at great cost to his self-respect. The soul-saving alternative that Jake selected, candidly telling his boss what he thought, cost him his position; unless he found another quickly—a difficult task his boss would not make any easier—he would not be able to care for his family, and his self-respect would be threatened along with everything else.

The moral contained in Jake's story became an important touchstone during my thirty years of marriage to Jewel Bell. Permanently ingrained in my memory is her predictable response whenever I sought her counsel before launching some protest that would likely jeopardize my job and outrage my colleagues. She would shake her head and sigh, "There you go again. After all these years, still trying to teach the white folks."

Jewel was not attempting to discourage my periodic crusades against what I deemed some manifestation of racist excess. She understood that the soul is sometimes sustained by action even when that action borders on the absurd. Rather, she was suggesting the difficulty and, often, the futility of trying to propagate my views about racial discrimination to those who already possessed quite different, and equally deeply held views about white entitlement. My heartfelt protests might annoy, but they would seldom undermine the authority or power of those I confronted. "Teaching the white folk" is thus both a manifestation of faith and an exercise in folly. I might believe that I was doing what I thought "right," but Jewel's admonition was a gentle reminder that I was not necessarily doing "good." That is, my good intentions might well translate into results that— at least in part—might be the very opposite of what I intended.

The discrepancy between doing what one thinks "right" and doing "good" can be applied profitably to an assessment of civil rights efforts over the last dozen or so years. Few will deny that the racial equality goals that a few decades ago seemed in sight are now further away than ever. Equality, experience tells us, did not follow the enactment of civil rights laws or victories in the courts. Similarly, the plight of the poor and the disadvantaged is not much eased by social programs, which no matter how ambitiously undertaken, seem able to deliver only food without nutrition, welfare without well-being, job training without employment opportunities, and legal services without justice. In fact, the minimum relief we provide to the needy serves mainly to dissipate the organizing and protesting potential generated by deprivation and thus ensures maximum status stability for the already well-off.

Risks, Rewards, and Reaffirmation

I am certain that when Thurgood Marshall argued in the school segregation decisions for an end to formal racial segregation, neither he nor the hundreds of civil rights advocates urging similar relief realized that the society was much more ready to move beyond Jim Crow signs and blatant racial exclusion than it was actually to provide equal opportunity and access without regard to race. We learned the hard way that commitment to white dominance could both survive official segregation and gain in effectiveness under the equal opportunity standard we civil rights lawyers had urged on courts and the country.

While earlier, blacks could be excluded simply because of their race, in the post-*Brown* world discrimination took a more subtle and more formidable form. Courts began finding that if a challenged rule or law did not overtly bar blacks, and if the rule was intended to further some arguably valid function, then civil rights challenges would fail in the absence of hard-to-obtain proof that the rule was intended or administered—despite its neutral language—to discriminate on the basis of race.[1] Proof that in its functioning the rule had the effect of excluding or burdening more blacks than whites was admissible but was not alone sufficient. Otherwise, as one Supreme Court opinion put it, civil rights suits "would raise serious questions about, and perhaps invalidate, a whole range of tax, welfare, public service, regulatory, and licensing statutes."[2] Even worse, rules enacted to help blacks are manipulated to preserve whites' interests at blacks' expense.[3]

Thus, rather than eliminate racial discrimination, civil rights laws have only driven it underground, where it flourishes even more effectively. While employers, landlords, and other merchants can no longer rely on rules that blatantly discriminate against minorities, they can erect barriers that, although they make no mention of race, have the same exclusionary effect. The discrimination that was out in the open during the Jim Crow era could at least be seen, condemned, and fought as a moral issue. Today, statistics, complaints, even secretly filmed instances of discrimination that are televised nation-wide—real estate agents steering black customers to black neighbor-hoods, schools relegating minority students to remedial tracks, and police officers harassing young black men—upset few people be-cause, evidently, no amount of hard evidence will shake the nation's conviction that the system is fair for all.

Given the intransigence of discrimination, civil rights campaigns aimed at changing the rules, without affecting the underlying status quo, have proved counterproductive even when their original goals were achieved. If this is paranoia, it is spurred and sustained by his-tory. Nor is it limited to racial issues. Doing good in this racially charged, economically disparate environment is not simply difficult, it may not be possible. As Jake's experience teaches, even those who are willing to risk their jobs in order to do good may invite disaster. Is it any wonder that racial reform efforts fail?

Given the existence of so many obstacles, the question posed by my late wife, Jewel, "Why does it always have to be you?", takes on new significance. As I have demonstrated, there is slight chance that a solo protest will either succeed itself or lead others to join the pro-test. On the other hand, the protest almost certainly will alienate those powers against whom it is aimed, and probably will harm, or at least upset, those on whose behalf it was undertaken. Those at a distance may applaud, but those close to the protester are likely to remain silent or be openly critical.

If you or people close to you are wronged, the only way to preserve your sense of self is to respond vigorously. The price of the challenge, though high, is often worth it. The writer Alice Walker told me that when she was still relatively unknown, a major magazine commis-sioned her to write an autobiographical piece about growing up in the deep South. Publication would, she knew, not only bring her writing to a national public but also provide a substantial amount of much-needed money. The magazine's editors, after perusing her manuscript, met her for lunch at an expensive New York restaurant, where they insisted on changes that she felt altered the character—as well as the accuracy—of her piece. Walker discussed her reservations about what they wanted, but the editors were adamant. "Listen to us, Alice," one of them finally told her with some exasperation. "If you want us to publish your article, you *have* to make these changes." Walker gathered together her manuscript and stood up to leave. "Listen to me," she told them, "all I *have* to do in life is save my soul."

Obviously, her determination to protect her integrity as a writer did not destroy, and almost certainly enhanced, the success Alice Walker later achieved. Surely, she knew that for anyone, but particularly for a black woman writing about race, a commitment to guarding one's artistic integrity at all costs is both essential and extremely difficult. The rewards for those blacks willing to tell whites only what they want to hear have always been both a temptation and a destructive trap.

But the need to confront authority knows no racial limits, nor is the willingness to do so a character trait that manifests itself only when one's job or career is on the line. Every day, in countless ways, people endure without response the affronts we all encounter. Tolerance may be a prerequisite for life in a civilized society, but those who make it a rule to let the small indignities pass without complaint can become so worn down by their treatment and so conditioned to remain silent that they will find themselves unable to fight the more serious battles. Far from insignificant, it is the willingness to take on the small challenges of daily life that prepares one to take a stand when people's basic rights are threatened.

Everyone knows firsthand the frustration of standing in a long, slowly moving line, whether it be at the bank, the supermarket, or any government agency issuing licenses, permits, and—especially— any form of public assistance. The scenario is familiar. One lone person is working at a counter designed for several clerks. At the bank, most of the tellers' windows are vacant. At the market, the check-out aisles are closed. The tellers are checking their receipts. Cashiers, if present at all, are stocking shelves. Sometimes those who might be aiding long-waiting standees are huddled over in a corner gossiping, seemingly oblivious of the ever-lengthening line of unhappy customers. Every now and then—not invariably, you understand—but occasionally, when I find myself in such a line, my patience exhausted, I will take a deep breath and speak out in a firm voice: "Attention, management. We have all been waiting in this line for a very long time. We would appreciate you doing something to speed things up. Thank you very much." Almost always, in reluctant response to my loud call for service, three things will happen. First, those near me in line will disassociate themselves from me. They will turn away, avert their eyes, even take a step or so away, whatever they think necessary to indicate to others that they are not my companions in this disturbance. It is not they who are making a scene out of so ordinary an inconvenience as standing in a slow-moving line. Second, a manager or someone in charge will appear, offer an apology or explanation for the delay, and request that more booths be opened. The line begins to move more speedily. Third, at least one person in the line, after glancing about to ensure none of the others are watching, will look toward me, make eye contact, and nod appreciatively. I smile back, acknowledging the thanks.

This little scenario reflects in microcosm the order of events in challenges to authority of much greater significance. On-the-spot protests to long lines, of course, involve no real confrontation with authority. Managers understand that unhappy customers can become former customers. But, unless a few of those customers are willing—usually without the support of their fellow sufferers—to register vigorous complaints, long lines and other annoyances become routine.

Yet, rather than risk challenging any authority—however benign—most people will defer to it. The typical reaction to the inconvenience and delay of a long line is not a protest to management, but passive acceptance. This response was dramatized in a television commercial touting a Caribbean vacation as an escape from the frustration and stress of urban living. It showed a prospective passenger standing in line at her bank. She is mightily upset with the teller who, in her view, is the cause of the long line. The woman is ready to explode with frustration, but calms herself by remembering that by that evening, she will be flying off on vacation. To calm her frazzled nerves, she savors in advance the Caribbean's beautiful weather and warm beaches. Then she realizes that the line has not moved during her reverie. She becomes furious, but again gains relief by reminding herself that by evening, she will be on the plane, fleeing from all such hassles. Watching that commercial, I remembered my even longer waits in bank lines in Jamaica and other Caribbean vacation sites. How, I wonder, will this woman handle her bank-line frustrations there? I wonder as well how she responds to the other, small annoyances we all encounter: the landlord who fails—despite repeated requests—to make much-needed repairs, or the doctor who keeps her waiting despite the fact that she made an appointment, carefully wedged into a very busy day. More important, how does she handle the more direct denials of her dignity and worth at her job? What if she is overworked and underpaid, passed over for promotion, even subjected to unwelcome sexual comments by her supervisor? Does she repress it all by thinking about her next Caribbean vacation? If she wanted to break her pattern of resigned acceptance of mistreatment, would she know when and how to do it? Would she know how to assess the risks and maximize the likelihood that her confrontation will bring a much-desired change in her treatment, in her status, in her well-being? In other words, if one is not born with the motivation to confront authority, can one acquire it? And if one has it, does it wither away if not exercised?

Protest is, as Gloria Steinem suggests in her book *Revolution from Within*, a form of revolt.[4] Self-esteem, Steinem maintains, is the most revolutionary of qualities. Obedience is created by systems and ideological constructs that weaken a person's belief in his or her own merit.[5] She quotes a civil rights worker, H. Jack Geiger, a physician and a prime spokesperson for the Physicians for Social Responsibility: "Of all the injuries inflicted by racism on people of color, the most corrosive is the wound within, the internalized racism that leads some victims, at unspeakable cost to their own sense of self, to embrace the values of their oppressors."[6] As the saying goes, in order to free the body, one must first free the mind. Those who value themselves will have the courage and sense of self-worth to demand to be treated fairly and respectfully. Whatever the response, the demand in itself is liberating.

This is a difficult feat even for those African Americans who have not only achieved much, but are seen to have done so. For example, Arthur Ashe, in his book, *Days of Grace: A Memoir*, written with Arnold Rampersad just before Ashe's untimely death, reports that long ago he made peace with his home state, Virginia, and the South, and adds:

> But segregation had achieved by that time what it was intended to achieve: it left me a marked man, forever aware of a shadow of contempt that lay across my identity and my sense of self-esteem. Subtly the shadow falls on my reputation, the way I know I am perceived; the mere memory of it darkens my most sunny days. I believe that the same is true for almost every African American of the slightest sensitivity and intelligence. . . . I don't want to overstate the case. I think of myself, and others think of me, as supremely self-confident. . . . Still, I also know that the shadow is always there; only death will free me, and blacks like me, from its pall.[7]

For a black man who achieved so much both as a tennis player, author, broadcaster, businessman, activist, and as a caring citizen, this is a remarkable statement. The mark of oppression that Ashe recognized is widespread, destructive to many, and poses a constant challenge to our sense of who we are. It is the source of so much of the pathological behavior that society identifies as virtually a genetic trait

Risks, Rewards, and Reaffirmation

of blacks, rather than the result of lifelong deprivation, exclusion, and the resulting self-hate. As its victims, blacks should be acutely aware of the causes of such behavior, and yet precisely because of the mark of oppression, we are often more unforgiving than whites.

The Pulitzer Prize–winning author James Alan McPherson tells a poignant story about his father, which reflects the tendency of blacks to condemn the antisocial behavior that results from racism while ignoring its causes.[8] McPherson's father, a master electrician in Savannah, Georgia, had destroyed his life with alcohol. For long years, McPherson hated his father and blamed him alone for failing his family. After becoming successful himself, McPherson was invited back to his hometown to present a prestigious lecture and sought through his speech to show that he had forgiven his father for the alcoholism he could still not understand or excuse.

After the lecture, a long-time friend admonished him: "I found it incredible, totally unbelievable, that you could remember *no* specific incidents of oppression, to yourself or others around you. It is *impossible* for you to have been born in the South of the forties and not have experienced specific incidents of racial oppression. You may have suppressed those experiences in your subconscious, but they happened." The friend continued: "You sharply forgot to mention that time and time again, your father had been unjustly denied an electrician's license—and he was the best. Yes, Mr. Mac was the best, or so my father and mother told me. My father and mother also told me, and my brother and sister, that the lily-white test administrators would never release your father's test results. This refusal by *white folks* to grant your father an electrician's license and release his test scores, along with scores of other rejections and humiliations—the inheritance of all black people—caused your father irrevocable pain. The pain may have even caused him to masquerade—as many unpleasantries have undoubtedly caused you to masquerade—his hostilities toward whites. He turned to drink for relief, you turn to ideas. . . . Those black folk who did not have other escape mechanisms, had to masquerade, or face the sure prospect of being blown to pieces, physically and psychologically. Believe me, your father's alleged status as the first black master electrician in Georgia came at a terrible drain on his inner resources. His effort to become an electrician, much less a master electrician, was a great leap from the abyss of despair."[9]

Revealing the frustrating nature of so much of the progress blacks have made over the years, McPherson reports that his brother, who had his father's genius for things electrical and mechanical, is a mechanic for a major airline. For years now, he has been the only black mechanic in his shop. He once expected to be promoted to foreman. He took the standardized tests and outscored his peers. The rule was changed to make the election of a foreman democratic. He played politics, made friends, did favors. Finally, a somewhat friendly white peer told him, "Mac, your only trouble is your father was the wrong color." After every new foreman is elected, McPherson reports that his brother still receives calls at his home during off hours. These calls are from his peers, and they need help with technical problems that they cannot solve. They ask, "Mac, what should we do?"[10]

The question, "What should we do?" is one more appropriately posed to the modern day Macs who have obtained positions, prestige, and influence denied to McPherson's father, his brother, and to millions of other blacks as well. Like it or not, we are the Timurs selected for the Citadel, representatives for those who didn't make it, couldn't make it. Yes, we even are the representatives for those who, because they lack our skills and opportunities, or who, robbed of the motivation and good fortune that helped us along the way, now don't care whether they make it or not.

We must not forget, particularly those of us who are "first blacks," that our elections, appointments, and promotions were not based simply on our credentials, ability, or experience. As important—likely more important—than merit is the fact that we came along at just the right time. My faculty position at Harvard is far from unique in this regard. It was clear that outstanding black lawyers, like those discussed in this book—Charles Houston, William Hastie, William Coleman—all deserved positions they were denied because they were black. For them, there were no Tamars in the Citadel. They, unlike those of us who made it into the academic ranks, had neither the thrust of the civil rights movement, nor the perhaps unconscious, but no less motivating mandate of the urban riots to parlay their talent into a position.

These facts do not deny individual accomplishment, they simply require recognition that every black person in this society—and far more whites than are willing to acknowledge it—achieved success with the aid of good luck, connections, or both.[11] What is the obligation then of black people who have achieved place, position, and prestige? It is simply not to forget that every step we take up the ladder provides white society with another example that what they wish to believe about racism's demise is actually fact. This knowledge should not discourage achievement, but should serve as a continuing challenge to do as much to help our people as our success unintentionally serves to worsen their plight.

My friend the Reverend Peter Gomes gave me the key to what I view as my obligation. He advised me back in 1980, as I was leaving Harvard to become dean of the University of Oregon Law School. "Derrick," he said, "as a dean, you must look in the mirror each morning and say, 'I am an evil.' For you will have authority and sometimes you will disappoint expectations you should reward and will reward those expectations you should disappoint. There is no way you can avoid such mischief. So, each morning upon arising, you must look at yourself in the mirror, and remind yourself, 'I am an evil.' Then you must ask, 'But today, can I be a necessary evil?'"

It did not take me long to learn that Gomes was sadly wrong about the authority available—for either good or mischief—to a law school dean. But his admonition is most appropriate for successful blacks whose success unintentionally makes life harder for the many blacks whom they would like to help. For all of us, each day provides another opportunity to become, as Peter Gomes would put it, "a necessary evil." That is, we must not become so caught up in career advancement that we fail either to remember ourselves or remind those in authority that our individual advancement is not synonymous with group progress.

This is a principal point in Judge A. Leon Higginbotham's open letter to Justice Clarence Thomas:

> When I think of your appointment to the Supreme Court, I see not only the result of your own ambition, but also the culmination of years of heartbreaking work by thousands who preceded you. I know you may not want to be burdened by the memory of their sacrifices. But I also know that you have no right to forget this history. Your life is very different from what it would have been had these men and women never lived. . . . This history has affected your past and present life.[12]

Higginbotham's strong admonition is applicable to a wider group of blacks who maintain that they did make it on their own and vigorously assert that the subordinate status of blacks is the result, not of racial discrimination, but of personal and group inadequacy. As we saw in the last chapter, even Paul Robeson, W. E. B. Du Bois, and Martin Luther King, generally regarded as heroes, were criticized severely by other black leaders for their harsh statements *against* white authority, which other blacks feared would worsen conditions for the black race. But blacks feel even more threatened by other blacks who, for whatever reason, take positions *supporting* authority. Robeson, Du Bois, and King were deemed to have "gone too far." But blacks who are thought to have "sold out" or "betrayed the race" by making statements about racial issues that comfort and reassure whites are condemned as traitors and "Uncle Toms." No one will deny that self-help is a component of programs and policies intended to rescue the millions of blacks mired in poverty and despair, but the assertion that the problems of the poor will be solved by self-help alone is such an extreme position it suggests that those blacks willing to make such arguments do so for the public attention they gain. Such individuals are particularly disturbing to successful blacks because we know that—to some extent—our achievements are grounded in a willingness to work for or otherwise identify with individuals and institutions whose racial policies are far from commendable.

Writer Jill Nelson makes clear how difficult it is to maintain one's ethical bearings in the job market. Describing a series of interviews at a major white newspaper that was considering her as a reporter, she reports:

> I've been doing the standard Negro balancing act when it comes to dealing with white folks, which involves sufficiently blurring the edges of my being so that white folks don't feel intimidated and simultaneously holding on to my integrity. There is a thin line between Uncle Tomming and Mau-Mauing. To step over that line can mean disaster. On one side lies employment and self-hatred, on the other, the equally dubious honor of unemployment with integrity. In the middle lies something like employment with honor, although I'm not sure exactly how that works.[13]

Given the tightrope act blacks must perform to make it in this country, those blacks who deny that race plays any part in our success or failure are involved—at the very least—in serious denial. And yet the alienation from the community that blacks who confront their communities suffer is disquietingly similar to the rejection suffered by those who confront authority. I confess that I have at times been quick to condemn black professionals who have opted for the easy road to success for minorities, namely, ignoring the continuing perversity of racism and acting as though the law is fair and color-blind. While authority figures with favors to grant reward blacks whose views serve to legitimate the society's rose-colored assumptions about race, motivations may be as complex for those who comfort as they certainly are for those of us who confront authority.

I have railed at the appointment of Justice Clarence Thomas, whose major qualification for replacing the late Justice Thurgood Marshall on the Supreme Court is his willingness to kick black folks when they are down. Because his votes and opinions in his first few terms on the Court have shown no more racial sensitivity than his pre-Court positions, Thomas is now publicly condemned even by some blacks who—despite his positions opposing affirmative action and condemning civil rights leaders—supported his nomination under the rubric: "give the brother a chance."[14] But just as confrontations with authority sometime produce unexpected, positive results, perhaps even Justice Thomas's regrettable performance will prove of some benefit to blacks he seems so willing to reject and who—in turn—have surely rejected him. At the least, Thomas's presence on the nation's highest Court provides black people with a continuing reminder that what many of us condemn as a serious deficiency in him is, as well, a constant temptation in us.

This willingness to seek instruction even in travesty comes naturally to the protester. In my case, while I have been a civil rights litigator, administrator, and for the last quarter of a century, a law professor and writer, I have really been a teacher. I have learned over the years that while knowledge and understanding of the law are important, they are secondary to the essence of teaching, which Peter Gomes defines as the ability "to communicate not only subject, but self."

Gomes, in one of his justly famous Sunday morning sermons, reminded the congregation of what we all know, that the memorable teachers in our lives hold that status even though we do not recall a single thing they taught us. Rather, we remember them as individuals who spurred us to learn on our own, both the subject matter and ourselves. Gomes quoted a description of such a great teacher in England about whom it was said, "He taught as a learner, led as a follower, and so set the feet of many in the way of life."

Risks, Rewards, and Reaffirmation

Gomes pointed to a plaque at the front of the Memorial Church erected in memory of Andrew Preston Peabody, the third Plummer Professor of Christian Morals at Harvard, who served in that post for thirty-three years during the nineteenth century. The plaque states that the Reverend Peabody was remembered as author, editor, teacher, and preacher, and as helper of all whom he met. His worth was summed up in the statement: "His precept was glorified by his example."

A marvelous model for a teacher, but what of the individual teacher-protesters who rise and, with all the odds stacked against them, challenge authority? How find a lesson in the hostility of those in power or the negative reactions from a great many whom one counts as allies, if not friends? Often, the lone protester—abandoned (or worse) by associates and unable to reach his or her goal—will feel less like a teacher than the mythical Sisyphus, forever pushing to the top of the mountain the rock that, upon nearing the heights, only rolls back down to the bottom. At a first reading of Sisyphus, it is hard to escape the despairing, existential angst that accompanies any realization of the futility of struggle. But the French philosopher Albert Camus puts a different face upon Sisyphus' tragic fate.[15] Rather than hopelessness, Camus sees incredible courage and even liberation in this timeless story. He sees strength in Sisyphus' course, not because Sisyphus continues to push the rock to the mountain's top, but because he returns to the bottom to retrieve it—knowing he will never get it to the top. "At each of those moments when he leaves the heights and gradually sinks toward the lairs of the gods, he is superior to his fate. He is stronger than his rock."

In appraising Sisyphus' dilemma, Camus has offered the protester cum teacher a lesson that transcends the bounds of philosophy and enters the realm of art. For, in the final analysis, art is an expression that provides a heightened meaning and appreciation of the human experience. The artist in the vanguard seldom works in an environment of acceptance. Faced often with rejection and ridicule, he or she pushes against the bounds of convention in an effort to create a new convention, sometimes building on, but more often exceeding and threatening accepted conventions.

Alice Walker opens her essay "Saving the Life That Is Your Own: The Importance of Models in the Artist's Life" with a letter to Emile Bernard from Vincent Van Gogh.

> However hateful painting may be, and however cumbersome in the times we are living in, if anyone who has chosen this hand-icraft pursues it zealously, he is a man of duty, sound and faithful.
>
> Society makes our existence wretchedly difficult at times, hence our impotence and the imperfection of our work. . . . I myself am suffering under an absolute lack of models. What I am doing is hard, . . . but that is because I am trying to gather new thoughts by doing some rough work, and I'm afraid ab-stractions would make me soft.[16]

Thus, Van Gogh captures in words the similarity of his work to that of the individual protester. Both seek to communicate the feelings of life and thereby more fully experience and give meaning and substance to one's existence. Just as the artist may hope for recognition, so the protester hopes that assertive action may bring about reform. Such hopes, though, supplement rather than fuel the main creative urge: expression of self through a medium—painting or protest—that communicates a view of "what is" against a background of *what might be.*

It was in that spirit that I presented what was to be my last speech to Harvard law students as a faculty member, early in 1992. At bottom, I reminded them, my protest leave was undertaken less to change the school than to influence students through example as well as through exhortations of perhaps the most important lesson my life experience has taught: commitment to change must be combined with readiness to confront authority. Not because you will always win, not because you will always be right, but because your faith in what you believe is right must be a living, working faith, a faith that

Risks, Rewards, and Reaffirmation

draws you away from comfort and security and toward risk, when necessary, through confrontation.

The underlying lesson in all my courses is that individuals must gain control of their lives, not by attaining riches or power or fame, but by confronting and trying to remedy a few of the evils and wrongs that we witness every day. The opportunity to illustrate my commitment to that belief has been worth the sacrifices I have made—which, in fact, have been few. I say this even if the warnings are borne out that my protest at Harvard in fact retards the progress toward diversity the faculty all claim to support in principle.

Daring to risk. That is tough. After all, there is at Harvard, as in the rest of our modern world, a distressing commitment to the unwritten commandment: "Thou shalt conform and not confront." The seeking of security seems to be a priority at Harvard, where faculty members are tenured, most key staff are equally secure, and students—compared to most of their counterparts around the country—are well off, indeed. In asserting the supremacy of the University, the members of its community are seldom meek or humble or submissive. Nor, in my experience, are they tolerant of those within their midst who dare venture beyond accepted procedures in an effort to bring change and reform. In this, the Harvard community is not significantly different from centers of power the world over.

Eventually, the Harvard Law School will hire and tenure its first woman of color. If my experience is a guide, even that event will not herald the adoption of policies intended to ensure either diversity or merit in the hiring process. It is even more certain that social reform, when it comes, at Harvard or elsewhere—will be borne on the scary wings of risk. In the very grasp of that fear, we must commit ourselves to reform, and retain that commitment while staring in the face of overwhelming evidence that the change we seek will be difficult—even impossible—to achieve.

Chiding the large group that had turned out for my talk, I reminded them that they must move beyond the trappings of reform—

attending rallies, applauding speeches, and enjoying the camaraderie of the moment. I warned them about equating their presence at these events with the kind of commitment that enables one to struggle for change that may not come and to persevere despite the opposition that will come. All of us, I advised, can learn from my enslaved forebears that in the commitment to living, to warding off oppressors, harassing them when we can, helping others, there is the stuff of triumph, recognizable even in defeat.

The analogy with slavery is less remote than it might appear. Like the slaves, law students—and likely a substantial portion of the citizenry in general—must live their lives under the debilitating weight of subordination and abuse—not physical certainly—but mental and emotional. The effort to get ahead or, at least, to hold one's own, extracts a fearful price in diminishing freedoms that are no less lost for being voluntarily surrendered.

Americans of all races have been in denial about our history of African slavery. Whites fear blacks will use it to provoke guilt, and blacks fear whites will use it to enhance their superior status. But lost in this collective amnesia is an uplifting example, one of great potential value in our modern world. Again, the enslavement of African peoples in this country was infinitely worse than anything that occurs at Harvard or elsewhere, but out of lives transformed by law into property, the slaves created models of fortitude and faith. The lives of this oppressed people and their legacy of music, art, and religion defy their awful condemnation to lives in bondage. They insisted on their humanity despite a hostile world's conviction that they were chattel, nothing more.

As the slave singers raised their voices to freedom, they must have known that there was no escape, no way out—in this world. The lyrics of their songs dreamed of a "City Called Heaven," but while they lived, they continued to engage themselves in the creation of humanity. Here is our model. We need do no more—and surely must do no less—than seek to emulate what they have done.

Risks, Rewards, and Reaffirmation

Because few in the Citadel ever betrayed their roles, there had been little need for the sacrifice of the sack, a humiliating form of banishment. In the last Council meeting he presided over alone, Xercis struggled between his devotion to the Citadel's laws and his love for his daughter. In the end, the Council of Elders rejected his pleas on Tamar's behalf. Unanimously—by the vote of all the Elders, including Timur—Tamar was condemned. The Council then compelled Xercis to select Timur, now the consummate insider-outsider, as his successor and thus his assistant in the banishment ritual whereby Tamar would be encased in the meanest sack and lowered from the Citadel's battlements.

Tamar accepted her fate, even welcomed it. She would miss her father, but she did not regret her commitment to the lowlanders. She did not have to travel far from the Citadel to find people to take her in. Still, she knew—as for the last time she looked back at the castle, its white walls gleaming in the moonlight—they would never accept her as one of them.

Many of the lowlanders sensed, rather than remembered, another era, an era long before this one when fair-skinned, straight-haired people like themselves had been dominant in the world. Then they had been the oppressors and those who now ruled from the Citadel with their dark skins and thick hair had been the oppressed. Now, deprived of the Citadel's power, Tamar knew that she would be shunned by some lowlanders and mistreated by others. Her resemblance to her ancient, African ancestors could outweigh all her good works on their behalf. Well, even in the Citadel, she had met distrust, not because of color, but because she was a woman, and because she challenged tradition by speaking out. It was her destiny, one she had made for herself. One she would continue to make on the unknown road ahead.

NOTES

Preface

1. Harry Edwards, *The Revolt of the Black Athlete* (1969). John Carlos and Tommie Smith, who raised black-gloved, clenched fists of black power in protest at a medal ceremony at the 1968 Olympics were themselves boycotted for years in sports and in the job market by outraged whites. See also Dick Gregory, *Nigger: An Autobiography* (1964), 192–93.

2. For accounts of civil rights protests and protesters, see, e.g., Henry Hampton and Steve Fayer, *Voices of Freedom: An Oral History of the Civil Rights Movement from the 1950s through the 1980s* (1990); Robert Weisbrot, *Freedom Bound: A History of the Civil Rights Movement* (1990); Taylor Branch, *Parting the Waters* (1988); David Garrow, *Bearing the Cross: Martin Luther King, Jr., and the Southern Christian Leadership Conference* (1986); Lerone Bennett, Jr., *Before the Mayflower: A History of Black America*, 5th ed. (1982).

3. Derrick Bell, "The Elusive Quest for Racial Justice: The Chronicle of the Constitutional Contradiction," in *The State of Black America, 1991*, ed. Janet Dewart (1991), 9.

Introduction

1. In addition to Regina Austin (University of Pennsylvania) and Anita Allen (Georgetown), who visited at Harvard, there is Patricia Williams (Columbia), Kimberle Crenshaw (University of California, Los Angeles), Linda Greene (Wisconsin), Mari Matsuda (Georgetown), and Lani Guinier (University of Pennsylvania).

   Richard Delgado and Jean Stefancic, "Critical Race Theory: An Annotated Bibliography," 79 *Virginia Law Review* 461 (1993), a bibliography of leading critical race theorists, also provides a glimpse of the number of women of color who are making important contributions in this new approach to legal scholarship. This list includes, along with the women listed above, Taunya Banks (Maryland); Robin Barnes (Connecticut); Paulette Caldwell (New York University); Adrienne Davis (University of San Francisco); Peggy Davis (New York University); Leslie Espinoza (Arizona); Angela Gilmore (Iowa); Trina Grillo (University of San Francisco); Angela Harris (Boalt Hall); Lisa Ikemoto (Indiana); Sheri Lynn Johnson (Cornell); Deborah Waire Post (Touro); Dorothy Roberts (Rutgers); Margaret Russell (Santa Clara); Judy Scales-Trent (Buffalo); Adrien Wing (Iowa). In all, there are two hundred minority women now teaching in American Bar Association accredited law schools and eleven thousand more in legal practice. "Black Women Find Law Rewarding: Despite Racism and Sexism, More African American Women are Entering the Legal Profession," *Orlando Sentinel Tribune*, 28 March 1992, E28.

Women have had a disproportionately hard time gaining entry into law school faculties. Bearing the double cross of race and gender, they have faced higher barriers and lower expectations of success. One study of minority law professors hired between 1986 and 1991 concluded that minority women fare even worse in law school hiring than minority men—who themselves have had no easy time. The women, whose credentials were virtually identical to those of the men in the study, were hired by less prestigious law schools and were more likely to teach low-status courses. Deborah J. Marritt and Barbara F. Reskin, "The Hidden Bias of Law Faculties," *Recorder*, 28 August 1992, 7.

2. In the first three years after my protest began, several white men and a few white women joined the faculty, but the school did not add a single, new diverse candidate. Two tenure-track black professors, Charles Ogletree and David Wilkins, both of whom were hired as assistant professors years before, were granted tenure, and another black professor, Scott Brewer, already hired to join the law school as an assistant professor, began teaching during this period. The remaining appointments were all white men and women.

Chapter One

1. Irvis was the plaintiff in *Moose Lodge No. 107 v. Irvis*, 407 U.S. 163 (1972), an unsuccessful challenge to the constitutionality of Pennsylvania's liquor

license regulations that permitted a private club to refuse to serve Irvis because he was black. In subsequent litigation in the state courts, Irvis gained a ruling that the club was a place of public accommodation under state law and thus could not exclude patrons on the basis of race. *Commonwealth v. Loyal Order of Moose, Lodge No. 107*, 294 A.2d 594 (Pa. 1972).

2. Hastie's experience in the War Department is chronicled in Phillip McGuire, *He Too Spoke for Democracy: Judge Hastie, World War II, and the Black Soldier* (1988). See also Gilbert Ware, *William Hastie: Grace Under Pressure* (1984).

3. McGuire, *He Too Spoke*, 12.

4. Ibid., 83.

5. Ibid., 84.

6. Ibid., 84–85, quoting editorial, *New York Amsterdam Star-News*, 6 February 1943.

7. Peter Bergman, *The Chronological History of the Negro in America* (1969), 516.

8. See *New York Times*, 15 October 1968, 53; *New York Times*, 29 October 1968, 43.

9. Dick Gregory, *Nigger: An Autobiography* (1964), 157.

10. Ibid., 157–58.

11. Carl Rowan, *Dream Makers, Dream Breakers: The World of Justice Thurgood Marshall* (1993), 237.

12. Ibid., 20–21; see also Juan Williams, *Eyes on the Prize: America's Civil Rights Years, 1954–65* (1987), 19–21.

13. Williams, *Eyes on the Prize*, 19.

14. *Brown v. Board of Education*, 347 U.S. 483 (1954).

Chapter Two

1. Howard A. Glickstein, "Law Schools: Where the Elite Meet to Teach," 10 *Nova Law Review* 541 (1986).

2. Among the cases Judge Carter argued are *Gomillion v. Lightfoot*, 364 U.S. 339 (1960) (gerrymandering scheme which excluded black voters from election district violates the Fifteenth Amendment); *NAACP v. Alabama, ex. rel. Patterson*, 357 U.S. 449 (1958) (right to free association protects NAACP from requirement that it disclose its membership lists);

NAACP v. Button, 371 U.S. 415 (1963) (ban on lawyers' solicitations may not be used to prohibit NAACP attorneys from assisting in racial discrimination cases); *Griffin v. County School Board*, 377 U.S. 218 (1964) (county which closed public schools rather than integrate them and continued to fund private, segregated schools violated equal protection rights of black students); *Brown v. Board of Education (Brown I)*, 347 U.S. 483 (1954) (declaring illegal "separate but equal" public schools for black and white children); *Brown v. Board of Education (Brown II)*, 349 U.S. 294 (1955) (requiring school boards to desegregate with "all deliberate speed").

3. A study confirmed that Carter's and Glickstein's experiences were and are typical. Robert J. Borthwick and Jordan R. Schau, in "Gatekeepers of the Profession: An Empirical Profile of the Nation's Law Professors," 25 *University of Michigan* J.L. Ref. 191 (1991), report that the single most important factor in selecting a law professor is whether or not the candidate graduated from an elite law school (p. 230). Five of the nation's almost two hundred law schools, Harvard, Yale, Columbia, the University of Chicago, and the University of Michigan, supply one-third of the law professors, with Harvard alone accounting for 13 percent of them (p. 226). Among the seven top ranked law schools, 85.2 percent of the professors graduated from one of these elite schools (p. 231). Sixty-one percent of the professors at the higher ranking schools had held a judicial clerkship (37 percent with a Supreme Court Justice), and 37 percent had never practiced law (p. 219).

4. Towards the end of his life, Dr. King came to realize that the civil rights gains he had worked to achieve would be meaningless without deeper social and, in particular, economic reform. See, e.g., Martin Luther King, Jr., "Where Do We Go from Here: Chaos or Community?" in *A Testament of Hope: The Essential Writings of Martin Luther King*, ed. James M. Washington (1986), 245–52, 614–17. See also David Garrow, "From Reformer to Revolutionary," in *Martin Luther King, Jr.*, ed. David Garrow (1984).

5. *Brown I*, 347 U.S. at 483.

6. See Derrick Bell, *And We Are Not Saved: The Elusive Quest for Racial Justice* (1987), 259 n. 6, which lists individual black law teachers at white schools in the pre-1969 era. For a detailed history of black lawyers and

law scholars, see J. Clay Smith, *Emancipation: The Making of the Black Lawyer 1844–1944* (1993).

7. Derrick Bell, "Application of the 'Tipping Point' Principle to Law Faculty Hiring Policies," 10 *Nova L. J. Review* 319 (1986).

8. William J. Wilson made this point in his book *The Declining Significance of Race* (1978), 110–11: "affirmative action programs are not designed to deal with the problem of the disproportionate concentration of blacks in the low-wage labor market. Their major impact has been in the higher-paying jobs of the expanding service-producing industries in both the corporate and government sectors." See also Randall Kennedy, "Persuasion and Distrust: A Comment on the Affirmative Action Debate," 99 *Harvard Law Review* 1327, 1333–34 (1986) [citing *Fullilove v. Klutznick*, 448 U.S. 448, 538 (1980), Stewart, J., dissenting] ("those who are the most disadvantaged . . . are the least likely to receive any benefit from . . . special privilege") and J. Leonard, *The Impact of Affirmative Action* (1983), 132. Stephen Carter raises the same point in *Reflections of an Affirmative Action Baby* (1991), 71–84.

9. John Osborne, *The Paper Chase* (1968).

10. My writing was at the forefront of a new school of legal thought now known, and mostly accepted, as critical race theory. Practitioners, often through storytelling and a more subjective, personal voice, examine the ways in which the law has been shaped by and shapes issues of race. Some of the most exciting and thought-provoking scholars today are part of this movement, including Regina Austin, Kimberle Crenshaw, Jerome Culp, Richard Delgado, Cheryl Harris, Charles Lawrence, Mari Matsuda, Kendall Thomas, and Patricia Williams.

11. Derrick Bell, *Race, Racism and American Law*, 3d ed. (1992).

12. Houston, elected to the *Harvard Law Review* in 1921, was the first black person to serve on that publication. J. Clay Smith, *Emancipation: The Making of the Black Lawyer, 1844–1944* (1993), 39, documents in great detail the history of the exclusion of blacks from law schools and law teaching.

13. The readings were entitled *The Legal Process: Basic Problems in the Making and Application of Law*.

14. The law holds that hiring criteria that disproportionately exclude minorities are illegal unless these criteria are proved to be job related.

Griggs v. Duke Power Co., 401 U.S. 424 (1971); see also *International Union, UAW v. Johnson Controls*, 499 U.S. 187 (1991); *Connecticut v. Teal*, 457 U.S. 440 (1982); *Dothard v. Rawlinson*, 433 U.S. 321 (1977). Employers must validate hiring standards which have a disparate impact on minorities, demonstrating that these standards actually predict a person's ability to perform the tasks required for the job, *and* that no other system would work as well without excluding so many minority candidates. In other words, the employer must show that its criteria are so related to performance that we must accept their exclusionary effect. Theoretically, all employers—even the most elite—are bound by this requirement. But see Elizabeth Bartholet, "Application of Title VII to Jobs in High Places," 95 *Harvard Law Review* 947 (1982), arguing that courts silently have relaxed the law as it applies to these high-level positions.

15. See "A Black Boycott at Harvard Law," *Newsweek*, 23 August 1982, p. 71; "Point of Hue: Racism Hits an Unlikely Victim," *Time* 23 August 1982, p. 48. The same course was forced out of Stanford Law School when minority students there protested against it. "Stanford Rights Class Dropped After Black Protest," *New York Times*, 20 March 1983, 27.

16. Luix Overbea, "More Minority Teachers at Harvard Law School, Black Students Demand," *Christian Science Monitor*, 24 December 1982, 18.

Chapter Three

1. Regina Austin, "Sapphire Bound!" 1989 *Wisconsin Law Review* 539 (1989).

2. The black woman, Crystal Chambers, sued her employer, the Girls Club of Omaha, for wrongful discharge and a number of related claims. Finding that the rule did not discriminate against black women, the court dismissed her suit. *Chambers v. Omaha Girls Club*, 629 F.Supp. 925 (D.Neb. 1986), *aff'd*, 834 F.2d 697 (8th Cir. 1987).

3. Austin, "Sapphire," 541.

4. *All the Women Are White, All the Blacks Are Men, but Some of Us Are Brave*, ed. Gloria Hull, Patricia Scott, Barbara Williams (1982).

5. Letter from Derrick Bell to Dean Robert Clark, 9 April 1993, on file with the author.

6. For a good anecdotal discussion of the reactions of both blacks and whites to affirmative action, see Studs Terkel, *Race: How Blacks and Whites Think and Feel About the American Obsession* (1992).

7. See, e.g., *New Negro Alliance v. Sanitary Grocery Co.*, 303 U.S. 552 (1938), where the Court found that federal labor law protected blacks picketing and urging a boycott against a grocery chain that did not employ black clerks against state court injunctions. But in *Hughes v. Superior Court of Cal.*, 339 U.S. 460 (1950), the Court upheld a state court injunction of a boycott to force a grocery chain to hire a percentage of blacks equal to the percentage of the chain's black customers on the grounds that it violated the state's fair employment policy. The cases are discussed in Derrick Bell, *Race, Racism and American Law*, 3d ed. (1992), § 6.10.

8. Charles V. Hamilton, *Adam Clayton Powell: The Political Biography of an American Dilemma* (1991), 95–105. See also Lerone Bennett, *Before the Mayflower* (1961), 360–61.

9. Executive Order 8802 (June 25, 1941), set out in *The Civil Rights Record 1970*, ed. Richard Bardolph, 301–2.

10. See *NAACP v. Claiborne Hardware Co.*, 458 U.S. 886 (1982). In 1966, the black residents of Port Gibson, Mississippi, presented civic and business leaders with a list of demands for racial equality and integration. Among them were the desegregation of public schools and facilities, the hiring of black police officers, the inclusion of blacks in jury pools, the improvement of black neighborhoods, and an end to verbal abuse by law enforcement. They also declared: "Negroes are not to be addressed by terms as 'boy,' 'girl,' 'shine,' 'uncle' or any other offensive term, but as 'Mr.,' 'Mrs.,' or 'Miss,' as is the case with other citizens" (at 899). When there was no satisfactory response from white authorities, the over five hundred people attending the local NAACP meeting voted unanimously to boycott the town's white businesses. The boycott lasted for six years, during which time some modest gains were made in hiring black employees and in other, more minor areas. The black citizens were remarkably united, and those who broke the boycott found that their names were read at NAACP meetings and published in a mimeographed newsletter, *Black Times*. In 1969, white merchants sued to recover damages for the business they lost and to enjoin the boycott in the future. After a trial, the organizers of the boycott were found liable for anti-trust and tort violations and assessed damages in the amount of

over $1 million. An injunction was also issued. The case eventually reached the Supreme Court, which overturned the judgment and held that the boycotters' activities were protected by the First Amendment.

11. For one of the most comprehensive accounts of the Montgomery bus boycott, see Taylor Branch, *Parting the Waters* (1988), 120–203.

12. Barbara Reynolds, *Jesse Jackson: America's David* (1985), 1, 9.

13. Isabel Wilkerson, "Challenging Nike, Rights Group Takes a Risky Stand," *New York Times*, 25 August 1990, 10.

14. Jonathan Tasini, "The Beer and the Boycott," *New York Times*, 31 January 1988, 19.

15. Glenn Fowler, "Civil Rights Groups and Coors Reach $325 Million Business Accord," *New York Times*, 19 September 1984, A18. For a discussion of other consumer boycotts, see Mark Stencel, "The Boycott Comes of Age; Firms May Not Always Meet Demands, but They Are Listening," *Washington Post*, 26 September 1990, F1; Anthony Ramirez, "From Coffee to Tobacco, Boycotts Are a Growth Industry," *New York Times*, 3 June 1990, 2.

16. Fox Butterfield, "Harvard Law Professor Quits Until Black Woman is Named," *New York Times*, 24 April 1990, A1; John H. Kennedy, "Harvard Black Eyes a Leave in Tenure Dispute," *Boston Globe*, 24 April 1990, 1.

17. Anthony Flint, "Rev. Jackson at Harvard Urges National Conference on Racism," *Boston Globe*, 10 May 1990, 1.

18. Letter to the Editor, *Boston Globe*, 4 May 1990.

19. Letter to the Editor, *Harvard Law Rec.*, 4 May 1990, 4.

20. Unpublished statement. Copy on file with author.

Chapter Four

1. Roger Fisher and William Ury, *Getting to Yes: Negotiating Without Giving In* (1981).

2. Lisa Lapin, "Calling for Diversity at Stanford," *San Jose Mercury News*, 2 May 1990, B1, B3; Tracie Reynolds, "Stanford Law School Solidarity Protest for Minority Hiring," *Peninsula Times Tribune*, 2 May 1990, B1.

3. These professors are Patricia King, Eleanor Holmes Norton, Emma Jordan, Anita Allen, Mari Matsuda, and Elizabeth Patterson.

4. Cheryl Harris, "Law Professors of Color and the Academy of Poets and Kings," 68 *Chicago-Kent Law Review* 331, 336–37 (1992).
5. Cheryl Harris, "Whiteness as Property," 106 *Harvard Law Review* 1710 (1993).
6. Sean Murphy, "Students Honor Law Professor as He Begins His Protest Leave," *Boston Globe*, 21 October 1990, 34.
7. See generally Elizabeth Bartholet, "Application of Title VII to Jobs in High Places," 95 *Harvard Law Review* 945 (1982) and cases cited therein. The Court of Appeals for the Second Circuit observed that "an anti-interventionist policy has rendered colleges and universities virtually immune to charges of employment bias, at least when the bias is not expressed overtly." *Powell v. Syracuse University*, 580 F.2d 1150, 1153 (2d Cir.), *cert. denied*, 439 U.S. 984 (1978). See also *Kumar v. Board of Trustees, Univ. of Mass.*, 774 F.2d 1 (1st Cir. 1985), *cert. denied*, 475 U.S. 1097 (1986); *Langland v. Vanderbilt Univ.*, 772 F.2d 907, 1985 WL 13611 (6th Cir., Tenn.); *Jamerson v. Board of Trustees of Univ. of Ala.*, 662 F.2d 320 (5th Cir. 1981); *Jackson v. Harvard University*, 721 F.Supp. 1397 (D.Mass. 1989), *aff'd*, 900 F.2d 464 (1st Cir.), *cert. denied*, 498 U.S. 848 (1990). Given the recent trend in Supreme Court decisions, which makes it even harder to prove employment discrimination, it is even less likely that a potential teacher would prevail. See, e.g., *St. Mary's Honor Ctr. v. Hicks*, 113 S.Ct. 2742 (1993) (holding that proof that an employer lied about the reason for firing the employee is not persuasive evidence that the firing was wrongful); *Wards Cove Packing Co. v. Atonio*, 490 U.S. 642 (1989), *aff'd in part, vacated in part*, 10 F.3d 1485 (9th Cir. 1993).
8. *Harvard Law School Coalition for Civil Rights v. President and Fellows of Harvard College*, Civil Action No. 90-7904-B (Super.Ct. Mass. 1991) (Brady, J.). In addition to the Coalition for Civil Rights there were eleven named student plaintiffs, who were also the attorneys of record: William Anspach, Christian Arnold, John Bonifaz, Keith Boykin, Pat Gulbis, Laura Hankins, Chris Jochnick, Lucy Koh, Jeffrey Lubell, Linda Singer, and Inger Tudor.
9. *Harvard Law School Coalition for Civil Rights v. President and Fellows of Harvard College*, 595 N.E.2d 316 (Mass. 1992).
10. Ken Myers, "Students Take Diversity Fight Against Harvard to State Court," *National Law Journal*, 4 March 1991, 4.

11. David M. Rabban, "Does Academic Freedom Limit Faculty Auton-
omy?" 66 *Texas Law Review* 1405, 1411 n.27 (1988), citing Kingman
Brewster, "On Tenure," 58 *AAUP Bulletin* 381, 382 (1972).

12. Ibid., 1411.

13. See, e.g., Elaine Mensh and Harry Mensh, *The IQ Mythology: Class,
Race, Gender, and Inequality* (1991). One New York court, for instance,
upheld charges that the SAT is biased against women and held that relying solely on these scores in awarding state scholarships violates the
law. *Sharif v. New York Educ. Dep't*, 709 F.Supp. 345 (S.D.N.Y. 1989).

14. Patricia J. Williams, *The Alchemy of Race and Rights* (1991), 84–85; see
also Derrick Bell and Erin Edmonds, "Students as Teachers, Teachers as
Learners," 91 *Michigan Law Review* 2025 (1993), discussing black students' reactions to exam question which asked students to analyze
whether a nephew could be disinherited because he was black.

15. Phoebe Haddon, "Academic Freedom and Governance: A Call for Increased Dialogue and Diversity," 66 *Texas Law Review* 1569 (1988).

16. The class preferences which color faculty hiring policies are no less
powerful in other areas of legal education. Historically, for instance, law
schools campaigned vigorously against the establishment of night
schools, which would open the profession to those unable to attend law
school because they had to work for a living.

17. See Bartholet, "Application of Title VII," 95 *Harvard Law Review* 947
(1982).

Chapter Five

1. Anita Allen, *Uneasy Access: Privacy for Women in a Free Society* (1988).

2. Memo from Dean Clark to Interested Members of the Law School Community, "The Timing of Offers to Visiting Professors," 5 March 1992.

3. Jack Sullivan, "Bell to Extend His Boycott Over Harvard Law Hirings,"
Boston Globe, 5 March 1992, 33.

4. "An Open Letter to the Harvard Law School Community," 20 April 1992,
signed by Elizabeth Bartholet, Gary Bellow, David Charny, Abram
Chayes, Christopher Edley, Martha Field, William Fisher, Charles Haar,
Morton Horwitz, David Kennedy, Duncan Kennedy, Frank Michelman,
Richard Parker, Lewis Sargentich, and Laurence Tribe.

5. Fox Butterfield, "Parody Puts Harvard Law Faculty in Sexism Battle," *New York Times*, 27 April 1992, A10. Unfortunately, the recommendations made by the letter's signers—formation of a new Appointments Committee and a resolution calling for diversity in the faculty—were little more than the same old pleadings, and would, in any event, do little to change things at the Law School.

Chapter Six

1. Derrick Bell, *Faces at the Bottom of the Well: The Permanence of Racism* (1992), 127.

Chapter Seven

1. Stanley Fish, *There's No Such Thing as Free Speech . . . and It's a Good Thing Too* (1994), 21.
2. John Kenneth Galbraith, *A Tenured Professor* (1990), 38–39.
3. Gerald Frug, "Argument as Character," 40 *Stanford Law Reveiw* 869 (1988).
4. Ibid., 887–88.
5. Jamin Raskin, "Laying Down the Law: The Empire Strikes Back," in *How Harvard Rules*, ed. John Trumpbour (1989), 341, 344–46.
6. Ibid., 344.
7. Ibid., 345.
8. These cases are discussed in Raskin, "Laying Down the Law," and Robert Weissman, "How Harvard is Ruled: Administration and Governance at the Corporate University," in *How Harvard Rules*, ed. John Trumpbour (1989).
9. Alice Dembner, "Harvard Law Ends Bias Suit by Agreeing on Institute," *Boston Globe*, 22 September 1993, 1.
10. Charles Peters and Taylor Branch, *Blowing the Whistle: Dissent in the Public Interest* (1972), 281–82.
11. Randall L. Kennedy, "Racial Critiques of Legal Academia," 102 *Harvard Law Review* 1745 (1989). Responses to Kennedy's piece were published in "The Legal Academy and Minority Scholars," 103 *Harvard Law Review* 1855 (1990).
12. Ian Haney-Lopez, "Community Ties, Race, and Faculty Hiring: The

Case for Professors Who Don't Think White," 1 *Reconstruction* 49, no. 3 (1991).

13. Ibid.

14. Patricia J. Williams, *The Alchemy of Race and Rights* (1991), 201.

15. Albert Camus, *The Rebel: An Essay on Man in Revolt* (1978), 8.

16. Ibid., 286–87.

17. Fox Butterfield, "Harvard Law School Torn by Race Issue," *New York Times*, 26 April 1990, A20.

18. See, e.g., Statement of Support for Professor Derrick Bell by Concerned Black Women Law Professors, March 1992; Emma Coleman Jordan and Charles Lawrence III, "The Law School Clone-O-Matic," *Legal Times*, 6 August 1990, 21–22.

19. See also Richard Delgado and Derrick Bell, "Minority Law Professors' Lives: The Bell-Delgado Survey," 24 *Harvard C.R.-C.L. Law Review* 349 (1989).

20. See "Black Women Law Professors: Building a Community at the Intersection of Race and Gender, A Symposium," 6 *Berkeley Women's Law Journal*, part 1 (1990–91), containing the reflections of black women law professors on my protest, their experiences as teachers, and their role in the academy.

   The half dozen articles contain very personal reflections on their law teaching experiences. While from a variety of different schools and subject matter areas, each woman reported resoundingly similar stories of being treated as less competent because of their race and gender. Students openly questioned their authority in the classroom, colleagues dismissed their work and their views, and administrators misunderstood and mishandled their troubles. Yet, as many of them described, these women of color have instructed, mentored, corrected, and exemplified perspectives and possibilities previously unrecognized in their schools. While the women disagreed on the reasons that should be advanced for their inclusion—role models, social justice, or "merit,"—all agreed upon the ultimate fact that women of color have not been, but must be, included in the legal academy.

21. Derrick Bell, *And We Are Not Saved: The Elusive Quest for Racial Justice* (1987), 198.

22. James Farmer, *Lay Bare the Heart: An Autobiography of the Civil Rights*

Movement (1985). Though fraught with violence, the Freedom Rides in 1961 were one of the most immediately effective protests of the civil rights movement. To stop the violence, Attorney General Robert Kennedy got the Interstate Commerce Commission to order the end of segregation in buses and terminals.

23. Ibid., 15–16.
24. Ibid., 106–7.

Chapter Eight

1. Theodore Rosengarten, *All God's Dangers: The Life of Nate Shaw* (1974), 332.
2. Frances Fox Piven and Richard Cloward, *Poor People's Movements: Why They Succeed, How They Fail* (1977), xx–xxi.
3. The phenomenon of group uprisings has been discussed in a wide range of theoretical contexts, from the psychology of Sigmund Freud to the sociology of Elias Canetti. See Sigmund Freud, *Group Psychology and the Analysis of Ego* (1959) and Elias Canetti, *Crowds and Power* (1963).
4. Two other women were convicted for incidents arising from their refusal to yield their bus seats, but neither was considered an appropriate vehicle for an all-out assault on segregation. See Taylor Branch, *Parting the Waters* (1988), 120–31.
5. Martin Duberman, *Paul Robeson* (1988), xiii.
6. Ibid., 222.
7. Ibid., 317–20.
8. Robeson was barred from appearing on NBC and became, according to Duberman, "the first American to be officially banned from television." Ibid., 384.
9. Paul Robeson, *Here I Stand* (1988), xxx.
10. Duberman, *Robeson*, 389. Robeson became one of only two United States citizens who could not even travel to non-passport destinations like Alaska and Puerto Rico.
11. Robeson, *Here I Stand*, 4.
12. Duberman, *Robeson*, 283.
13. Ibid., 360.
14. Walter White, Executive Director of the NAACP, for one, described

Robeson as a "bewildered man who is more to be pitied than damned."
Ibid., 394.

15. Ibid., 414.

16. Robeson, *Here I Stand*, 48.

17. Duberman, *Robeson*, 549.

18. See W. E. B. Du Bois, *The Autobiography of W. E. B. Du Bois* (1968).

19. Julius Lester, ed., *The Seventh Son: The Thoughts and Writings of W. E. B. Du Bois* (1971), 129–30, quoting W. E. B. Du Bois, who describes himself as "rejected of men."

20. Duberman, *Robeson*, 362.

21. Arthur Ashe, *A Hard Road to Glory: A History of the African-American Athlete Since 1946* (1988), 96, citing *Newsweek*, 15 July 1968, 57.

22. Or in words more characteristic of Ali:

> Keep asking me, no matter how long
> On this war in Viet Nam, I sing this song
> I ain't got no quarrel with the Viet Cong.

Jo Cottrell, *Man of Destiny: The Story of Muhammad Ali* (1967), 335, cited in Ashe, *A Hard Road*, 97–98.

23. Cottrell, *Man of Destiny*, 333–34. Sugar Ray Robinson claimed, though, that Ali had confided to him his real fear of going to jail. Ibid., 334.

24. Ashe, *A Hard Road*, 98.

25. Theodore Rosengarten, *All God's Dangers: The Life of Nate Shaw* (1974).

26. Nell Painter, *The Narrative of Hosea Hudson: His Life as a Negro Communist in the South* (1979); see also *Herndon v. Lowry*, 301 U.S. 242 (1937) (overturning conviction of black Georgian convicted of inciting insurrection by distributing Communist Party literature). The case is analyzed at length and in its historical context by Kendall Thomas in "*Rouge et Noir* Reread: A Popular Constitutional History of the Angelo Herndon Case," 65 *Southern California Law Review* 2599 (1992).

27. The list is long. It includes the following individuals, in addition to those mentioned elsewhere in the book: Sojourner Truth, a former slave who campaigned across the country for abolition, is the subject of Carleton Mabee, *Sojourner Truth: Slave, Prophet and Legend* (1993). Ida B. Wells and her crusade against lynching are chronicled in Ida B. Wells,

Crusader for Justice: The Autobiography of Ida B. Wells (1970); see also Dorothy Sterling, *Black Foremothers* (1979). Henry Hampton and Steve Fayer tell the stories of James Lawson, Unita Blackwell, and Aaron Henry, all of whom were organizers during the civil rights movement of the 1960s, in *Voices of Freedom: An Oral History of the Civil Rights Movement from the 1950's through the 1980's* (1990). Septima Clark and E. D. Nixon are featured in Eliot Wigginton, *Refuse to Stand Silently By: An Oral History of Grass Roots Social Activism in America, 1921–1964* (1991). Ivory Perry, a local organizer in St. Louis, is featured in George Lipsitz, *A Life in the Struggle: Ivory Perry and the Culture of Opposition* (1988). Carl Rowan tells of the Reverend L. Frances Griffin, who worked toward integrating the schools in Prince Edward County, Virginia, in *Dream Makers, Dream Breakers: The World of Justice Thurgood Marshall* (1993), 237–40. In *A Time to Die* (1975), Tom Wicker wrote of the Attica prison inmates who challenged the conditions of their confinement. Countless other individuals and stories have been memorialized.

28. The fury triggered when Daniel Ellsberg, a former government official, released secret documents exposing the government's duplicity in its Vietnam War policy, revealed the same tendency. The debate which followed centered not on the substance of Ellsberg's disclosures, but on the propriety of breaching national security rules in disclosing the "Pentagon Papers." As reporter Taylor Branch noted: "The political Left . . . talked about freedom, while the Right talked about rules. Nobody talked much about the war." Charles Peters and Taylor Branch, *Blowing the Whistle: Dissent in the Public Interest* (1972), 240.

29. David Garrow, *Bearing the Cross: Martin Luther King, Jr., and the Southern Christian Leadership Conference* (1986), 546–47, 551, 554.

30. Ibid., 555.

31. Ibid., 576–77, citing Carl T. Rowan, "Martin Luther King's Tragic Decision," *Reader's Digest*, September 1967, 37–42.

32. Ibid., 553, quoting editorial, *Washington Post*, 6 April 1967.

33. Ibid., 555–56.

34. Garrow, *Bearing the Cross*, 564.

35. James M. Washington, ed., *A Testament of Hope: The Essential Writings of Martin Luther King* (1986), 299.

36. Stanley Milgram, *Obedience to Authority: An Experimental View* (1974).

37. Ellsberg's experiences are recounted in an interview with Taylor Branch reported in Peters and Branch, *Blowing the Whistle*, 240.
38. Ibid., 254, 256.
39. Ibid.
40. Martin Luther King, "Letter from a Birmingham Jail," in Washington, *A Testament of Hope*, 295.
41. Copy of letter from Karen Fields to the Rochester University community, 1 May 1992 (on file with author).
42. For two major accounts of whistleblowing, see Myron Glazer and Penina Glazer, *Whistleblowers: Exposing Corruption in Government and Industry* (1989), and Peters and Branch, *Blowing the Whistle*. See also Lynn Bernabei, "Bill Pending in Congress Would Give Needed Federal Protection to Whistleblowers," *Manhattan Lawyer*, 10–16 May 1988, 3.

  According to a survey of 161 whistle-blowers published in the *Public Administration Review*, nearly three-fifths of federal whistleblowers lost their jobs, all had spent an average of $28,166 defending themselves, and about one-third had sought psychiatric counseling. "Whistleblowers' Sad Tune," *Government Executive*, February 1990 (citing *Public Administration Review*, Nov./Dec. 1989).

  Hundreds of cases are filed by individuals fired from their jobs for challenging corporate or government actions, and many of these individuals find no protection from either the government or the courts. See, e.g., Senate Committee on Government Affairs, *The Whistleblowers: A Report on Federal Employees Who Disclose Acts of Governmental Waste, Abuse, and Corruption*, S. Rep., 95th Cong., 2d Sess. 20 (1978), and cases cited in Bruce D. Fong, "Whistleblower Protection and the Office of Special Counsel: The Development of Reprisal Law in the 1980s," 40 *American University Law Review* 1015 (1991); Martin H. Malin, "Protecting the Whistleblower from Retaliatory Discharge," 16 *University of Michigan J. L. Ref.* 277 (1983); *NLRB v. Local Union No. 1229*, Int'l Bhd. of Elec. Workers, 346 U.S. 464 (1953) (upholding dismissal on loyalty grounds of technicians who distributed handbills attacking the quality of a television station's programming); *Novotny v. Great Am. Fed. Sav. & Loan Ass'n*, 539 F.Supp. 437 (W.D.Pa. 1982) (upholding firing of secretary who sided with employees in dispute with corporate president by confronting president in employees' presence);

Maus v. National Living Ctrs., Inc., 633 S.W.2d 674 (Ct. App. Tex. 1982) (nurse's aide fired for complaining about the neglect of patients not protected); but see, e.g., *Palmateer v. International Harvester Co.*, 421 N.E.2d 876 (Sup. Ct. Ill. 1981) (recognizing cause of action for employee fired for reporting the criminal activity of colleagues to law enforcement).

43. Silkwood's story is told, briefly, in Glazer and Glazer, *Whistleblowers*.
44. See Thomas Devine and Donald Aplin, "Whistleblower Protection—The Gap Between the Law and Reality," 31 *Harvard Law Review* 223 (1988).
45. The story of Fannie Lou Hamer is told by Kay Mills in *This Little Light of Mine: The Life of Fannie Lou Hamer* (1993).
46. Ibid., 51.
47. Ibid., 90–91.
48. Ibid., 303.

Chapter Nine

1. See, e.g., *St. Mary's Honor Ctr. v. Hicks*, 113 S.Ct. 2742 (1993) (proof that employer gave a false reason in justifying dismissal of employee is not proof that the motivation was racial; employee must find direct evidence that race motivated the dismissal); *Lorance v. AT&T Technologies, Inc.*, 490 U.S. 900 (1989) (operation of racially neutral seniority system which favored men over women is not unlawful without proof of discriminatory intent); *Wards Cove Packing Co. v. Atonio*, 490 U.S. 642 (1987), *aff'd in part, vacated in part*, 10 F.3d 1485 (9th Cir. 1993) (rejecting overwhelming statistical evidence that hiring policies restricted nonwhite workers to low-paying manual jobs as insufficient evidence of discrimination); *McCleskey v. Kemp*, 481 U.S. 279 (1987) (statistical evidence that racial discrimination plays a role in determining whether capital punishment is imposed does not invalidate petitioner's death sentence).
2. *Washington v. Davis*, 426 U.S. 229, 248 (1976).
3. See, e.g., *Wygant v. Jackson Bd. of Education*, 476 U.S. 267 (1986) (bargaining agreement's layoff provision, which softened effect of seniority clause on minority teachers who had been the last hired, was an imper-

missible racial classification); *Richmond v. J.A. Croson Co.*, 488 U.S. 469 (1989) (holding that voluntary set-asides of city contracts for minority businesses, when fewer than 5 percent of contracts are awarded to blacks in a city which is 50 percent black, unlawfully discriminates against whites); *Regents of the Univ. of Cal. v. Bakke*, 438 U.S. 265 (1978) (holding that an affirmative action program which gives weight to the race of the applicant, in order to increase minority admission, violated the equal protection rights of a rejected, white applicant).

4. Gloria Steinem, *Revolution from Within* (1992).

5. In *Revolution from Within*, Steinem argues: "The idea of intrinsic worth is so dangerous to authoritarian systems (or to incomplete democracies in which some groups are more equal than others) that it is condemned as self-indulgent, selfish, egocentric, godless, counter-revolutionary and any other epithet that puts the individual in the wrong" (68–69).

6. Ibid., 118.

7. Arthur Ashe and Arnold Rampersad, *Days of Grace: A Memoir* (1993), 127–128.

8. James Alan McPherson, "Going Up to Atlanta," in *A World Unsuspected: Portraits of Southern Childhood*, ed. Alex Harris (1987), 78.

9. Ibid., 104.

10. Ibid., 105.

11. Christopher Jencks makes this point at the conclusion of his study of education in America, *Equality: A Reassessment of the Effect of Family and Schooling in America* (1972), 226–28.

12. A. Leon Higginbotham, Jr., "An Open Letter to Justice Clarence Thomas From a Federal Judicial Colleague," 140 *University of Pennsylvania Law Review* 1005, 1007 (1992).

13. Jill Nelson, *Volunteer Slavery* (1993), 10.

14. See Trevor Coleman, "Doubting Thomas," *Emerge*, November 1993, 39. The cover photograph depicts Thomas with a handkerchief placed on his head via computer artistry. Joining a litany of black critics, William T. Coleman, Jr., a partner in a leading law firm and former Secretary of Transportation in the Ford administration, said, "It is sad. Justice Thurgood Marshall was a tremendous justice and made a tremendous contribution, and people would have hoped that this particular person who went through the doors he opened would act differently. Whatever

Thomas got in life, he got because Marshall fought like Hell to get him in the doors and you would think some people would have respect for those traditions" (42).

15. Albert Camus, *The Myth of Sisyphus and Other Essays* (1955).

16. Alice Walker, *In Search of Our Mothers' Gardens* (1984), 3–4. Van Gogh's letter explains that he had just completed five canvases of olive trees.

INDEX

Affirmative action, 47, 51, 78, 95,
    96, 139; opposition to, 33, 58,
    85, 86, 118, 140, 160
AFL-CIO, 60
African Methodist Episcopal
    church (AME), 15
Ali, Muhammad, 131–32,
    180nn22,23
Allen, Anita, 72, 83–84, 85, 87,
    167n1, 174n3; *Uneasy Access*, 83,
    176n1
Anheuser-Busch, 60
Anspach, William, 175n8
Aplin, Donald, 183n44
Appointments Committee, 37, 47,
    53, 54, 60, 88; and Scott Brewer,
    79; and Randall Kennedy, 84;
    rejection of Regina Austin by,
    82–83
Arnold, Christian, 175n8
Ashe, Arthur, 180n21; *Days of
    Grace* (with A. Rampersad), 154,
    184n7
Atomic Energy Commission, 141
Austin, Regina, 57, 64–65, 87,
    167n1, 171n10; effect of
    author's protest on, 114–15,

116, 118, 119; "Sapphire
    Bound!" 53–54, 116, 172n1;
    tenured position at Harvard Law
    School not offered to, 65, 72,
    82–84; as visiting scholar at
    Harvard Law School, 50–55

Banks, Taunya, 168n1
Bardolph, Richard, 173n9
Barnes, Robin, 168n1
Bartholet, Elizabeth, 172n14,
    175n7, 176nn17,4
Baseball, breaking of color barrier
    in, 131
Bator, Paul, 37
Bell, Ada Childress (mother), 10–
    11, 13, 14
Bell, Charles (brother), 11
Bell, Derrick, 171n7, 172n5,
    176n14, 178nn18,19; *And We
    Are Not Saved*, 117, 170n6,
    178n21; "Chronicle of the 27th
    Year Syndrome," 117–18; "The
    Elusive Quest for Racial Justice,"
    167n3; *Faces at the Bottom of the
    Well*, 177n1; *Race, Racism and
    American Law*, 171n11, 173n7

187

hiring and promoting faculty at, 76–80

Harvard School of Design, 139

Harvard University, 4, 6, 94, 107, 122; Black Faculty and Administrators of, 139; sex discrimination complaint filed against, 109

Hastie, William H., 17, 20, 40, 119, 157; his experience in War Department, 18–19, 25, 169n2

Health, Education, and Welfare, Department of, 24

Henry, Aaron, 181n27

Higginbotham, A. Leon, Jr., 158, 184n12

Horwitz, Morton, 108, 176n4

House Committee on Un-American Activities (HCUAA), 129, 130

Houston, Charles, 17, 40, 119, 157, 171n12

Howard Law School, 31, 44

Hudson, Hosea, 132, 180n26

Hull, Gloria, 172n4

Ikemoto, Lisa, 168n1

Irvis, Catherine, 16

Irvis, K. Leroy, 16, 168n1

Jackson, Jesse, 59, 63

Jencks, Christopher, 184

Jochnick, Chris, 175n8

Johnson, Sheri Lynn, 168n1

Jones, Paul, 15

Jordan, Emma Coleman, 174n3, 178n18

Jordan, Marian, 19–20

Justice, U.S. Department of, 17, 19, 20–21, 29; Civil Rights Division of, 18, 30, 112–13

Kennedy, David, 176n4

Kennedy, Duncan, 63, 103, 104, 176n4

Kennedy, John F., 39

Kennedy, John H., 174n16

Kennedy, Randall L., 47, 84, 110–11, 171n8, 177n11

Kennedy, Robert, 179n22

Kenyatta, Muhammed, 46

Kerr-McGee nuclear power plant, 141

King, Martin Luther, Jr., 6, 56, 131, 135, 138, 158; assassination of, 23, 32, 62; his Letter from a Birmingham Jail, 106, 135, 138, 182n40; and need for socioeconomic reform, 170n4; his opposition to Vietnam War, 133–34, 144

King, Patricia, 174n3

Koh, Lucy, 175n8

Korean War, 127

Lambda Legal Defense Fund, 74

Landers, Renee, 97

Lapin, Lisa, 174n2

Lawrence, Charles, III, 69–70, 171n10, 178n18

Lawson, James, 181n27

Lawyers Committee for Civil Rights Under Law, 74

Legal Defense and Educational Fund (LDF), 20, 21, 24, 46, 113

Leonard, J., 171n8

Index